MW01070635

Ready For Rapture

Total Surrender And Adoration

by

Susan Davis

Prophetic Messages Dictated To

Susan Davis

(July 2013 to September 2014)

ISBN-13: 978-1502718549

ISBN-10: 1502718545

TABLE OF CONTENTS

ABOUT THESE PROPHECIES

Susan operates in the gift of prophecy. In 1 Corinthians 14:1 it states, **"Follow the way of love and eagerly desire gifts of the Spirit, especially prophecy."** Now we are living and supposed to be obeying God's instructions in the New Testament. Although some believe that spiritual gifts, such as prophecies, have been done away with, this is man's thinking and not God's. God has not changed His covenant. We are still living in the era of the New Covenant – which is also called the New Testament. Please understand that your first commitment should be to the Lord Jesus Christ and His Word as written in the Bible – especially the New Testament.

As always, all prophecy needs to be tested against the Bible. However, if the prophecy lines up with the Bible then we are expected to obey it. Currently God does not use prophecies to introduce new doctrines. They are used to reinforce what God has already given to us in the Bible. God also uses them to give us individual warnings of future events that will affect us.

Just like in the Old Testament, God uses prophets in the New Testament times of which we are currently in. The book of Acts, which is in the New Testament, mentions some of the prophets such as Judas and Silas (Acts 15:32) and Agabus (Acts 21:21) and there were others. The ministry of prophets is also mentioned in New Testament times in 1 Corinthians 12:28, 14:1,29,32,37 as well as in Ephesians 2:20,3:5,4:11.

Jesus chooses prophets to work for Him on earth. Among other things, Jesus uses prophecies and prophets to communicate His desires to His children. The Bible itself was written prophetically through the inspiration of the Holy Spirit.

Some people say words of prophecy are in danger of adding to the Bible or taking from it -- well the Bible speaks of prophecy as being a Gift of the HOLY SPIRIT. The way the Bible is added to or taken from is not through additional words of prophecy received by the people which the HOLY SPIRIT gives words to, but by the changing of GOD's concepts to add new unBiblical concepts from other pagan beliefs for example. But the primary work of the prophets in the Bible has always been to focus the people back to GOD's WORD, the BIBLE.

As it says in 1 Thessalonians 5:19-21, **"Do not put out the Spirit's fire; do not treat prophecies with contempt. Test everything. Hold on to the good."** And the way to test the messages is to compare it's content to what the Bible says.

In all the prophecies below I personally (Mike Peralta - Book Preparer) have tested these messages and they are all in agreement to what the Bible says. But you must also test these messages, yourself, to the Bible. And if they are consistent with the Bible, then God expects that you will take them to heart and obey His instructions.

INTRODUCTION

INTIMACY WITH JESUS

The following introduction to Susan's book is a blog by Rob Rennie which gives a very good summary of what Jesus is calling us to do, in getting close to Him and to be counted worthy for the rapture and for heaven. Please read, understand, and obey. It is a great deal more important than you may currently realize.

==

(Used By Permission)

Posted on Aug 22, 2012 in The Supernatural Blog by Rob Rennie

http://www.eternalplanner.com/who-is-jesus-going-to-take-with-him/

Who is Jesus Going to Take With Him?

The ever-present question, whether you're a Christian, or not is, "How do you get into Heaven?' which is really, 'Who is Jesus going to take with Him to Heaven?'

Getting into Heaven, according to God's Word, is not an easy task. In fact, only few will enter.

The Bible also says, **"Many will say to me on that day, 'Lord, Lord, did we not prophesy in your name, and in your name drive out demons and perform many miracles?' And then will I profess unto them, I never knew you: depart from me, ye that work iniquity."**

This is probably one of the most, if not the most, sobering warnings in the Bible regarding getting into Heaven. If even the people who've called themselves Christians in this life, who've worked miracles in Jesus' name may not be going, then the number who will actually enter in seems to be critically low.

But the key to this whole passage lies in the verse directly preceding the warning, in Matthew 7:21. **"Not every one that saith unto me, Lord, Lord, shall enter into the kingdom of heaven; but he that doeth the will of my Father which is in heaven."**

Question: "Who is Jesus going to take with Him to Heaven?"

Answer: "The one who does the will of the Father. The key is doing the Father's will!"

How do you find out what the Father's will is? Recently, I've come across a fantastic book called, "Marriage Supper of the Lamb" by Susan Davis. She has a website that discusses the end times and the rapture.

Susan Davis happens to be one of those people who can really hear the Lord amazingly well and she regularly gets entire letters and in the case of this book, entire manuscripts dictated to her by the Lord.

In the book, the Lord tells her about how the people should prepare for the Rapture and for eternal life in general. The main point the Lord makes is that we should be 100% living for the Lord and that anything less than 100% is considered 'lukewarm' and will result in eternal damnation.

By the way, if you're skeptical about whether these revelations are really from the Lord, as you should be because we are supposed to test the spirits, I urge you to look at other testimonies by various other people around the world and compare the syntax and style with the content in the letters dictated to Susan. What you'll find is they are near identical and they in no way contradict the Word of God.

Anyhow, getting back to knowing God's will, the first thing we have to realize is that God doesn't expect us all to become ordained and start a church because as the verse above states, it's not about that and many of the people who do this are still going to hell because they've overlooked one critical fact.

The critical fact that nearly everyone is missing is that they don't spend enough intimate time with the Lord ! **How can you possibly know what the Lord's will is if you don't spend time with Him?** This is why the Lord says in the above verse, 'I never knew ye," keyword, "knew" meaning to actually know someone from having spent time with them.

Who is Jesus to you? If Jesus is nothing more than a historical figure to you, or a concept, or an idea, than you obviously don't know the Lord Jesus and your soul is in danger.

The first thing you have to recognize is that Jesus/Holy Spirit/God (to be used interchangeably) is spirit and that He is a living God. He is also a relational God and He created you to be intimate with Him. This means you were created to know God on a personal level, through prayer, reading your Bible, and spending time with God every day away from all the distractions of the world.

The moment you allow the cares of the world to supersede your number one priority, which should be to follow God's will, you show

11

yourself to be full of pride, thinking that you know better than God when it comes to how you should live your life.

How could you know better than God when it was God who created you and in fact created your life?? The Word of God says the Lord has designs for your life, plans to prosper you, not to hurt you. We can't even comprehend the destruction that we create by ignoring God's will, which is really the destiny that God has for us.

This is why being out of step with God's will is rebellion to God and what I would call the number one pitfall for every human being on earth and unfortunately, falling into it means you have more in common with satan than you do with God. This is why it leads people to hell.

How in the world are we supposed to spend intimate time with God if He's spirit and not physical?? Okay, calm down. Everything is going to be okay. If you're feeling uneasy or unsure about whether you'll be going to Heaven or not, I'm going to walk you through what you can start doing today in order to learn how to spend intimate time with God, learn what His will, or destiny is for your life and be with Him forever in Heaven.

*Note: And remember, just because God isn't physical doesn't mean He's not real, or has a presence that you can feel and a personality that you can get to know.

1) Set aside time every morning to pray to God and spend time with Him.

Ask Him what His will for your life is for that particular day and then do it. Do this every morning. If you do this, He will make Himself known to you and He will start speaking to your heart. You won't necessarily hear His answers, but you will feel them, especially if you do this regularly and learn how to be in God's presence and discern His voice.

2) Let God in on what you're thinking/experiencing/feeling every moment of the day.

Sometimes, we forget that God is always watching us, so we do things we know we shouldn't do. This is why it's good to always remind yourself that God really is watching over us, not in a creepy voyeuristic kind of way, but in a concerned parent kind of way. I like to have a running dialogue with God throughout the day, sharing my thoughts and opinions on different things and checking with Him to see if I'm in sync with Him or not. No matter what I'm doing, whether it's lifting weights, watching a movie, or spending time with friends, thinking about making a big decision in my life, I include God in every thing I do. If you do this, you'll find that there are many ways God speaks to you.

3) Read the Word on a regular basis.

This is something I have to get better about, but the reason you read the Word is quite simply to get to know what God's personality is like and what He expects from us. You get to know God by knowing what He says and what He does, just like you would a person. It just so happens that the Bible is a record of the things God says and what He does, so it's important that we read it. Ask the Holy Spirit to reveal certain things in the Bible to you which may at first glance seem complex. That's what the Holy Spirit is for.

Okay, now what? Once you've done that, you should be well on your way to having an intimate relationship with the Lord, but you have to work at it, just like everything else.

If you don't hear God speaking to you the very first time, don't just give up. Keep pursuing God's face.

One of the things that creates a division between us and God is sin, so make sure you repent of all your sin. If you're not sure what you have to repent for, ask God and He'll tell you in the form of mental pictures, words, or feelings.

Something else that I emphasize on this blog is the need to do prayer intercession to cut through the thick blanket of evil that exists in so many places around the world. Intercession is where you pray without ceasing until, in the spirit, you breakthrough this blanket and at that point, have a much easier time being intimate with God. Without all the demonic distractions and such.

EXERCISE:

Next chance you get, wake up, brush your teeth and then grab a piece of paper and a pencil. Sit down on the ground, raise your hands up to the sky and pray to God. Throughout the course of this prayer, you should ask God what His will is for you. When He tells you what it is, make sure you write it down. Then do it! Simple as that. Rest easy in the knowledge that God's perfect will consists of the decisions you yourself might make if you were all-knowing and all-powerful and had knowledge of the future. Since you can't really hold a candle to any of that, the smartest thing you can do is trust God's will for your life knowing He wants the best for you.

============== End Of Blog By Rob Rennie ==============

Prophetic Messages Through Susan Davis

1. IS YOUR WILL FOLLOWING THE ENEMY OF GOD OR GOD?

The LORD's Words for Today

Dear Followers of CHRIST:

John: 8:44: Ye are of your father the devil, and the lusts of your father ye will do. He was a murderer from the beginning, and abode not in the truth, because there is no truth in him. When he speaketh a lie, he speaketh of his own: for he is a liar, and the father of it.

Matthew 7:21 (KJV): Not everyone that saith unto ME, LORD, LORD, shall enter into the kingdom of heaven; but he that doeth the Will of MY FATHER which is in heaven.

These scriptures show that there are only two wills: GOD's or satan's. So the question for you is your will following the enemy of GOD or GOD?

I point this scripture out because of something the LORD revealed to me recently for the purpose of sharing with others: If you do not belong to GOD because you are not fully sold out to HIM and completely dead to "self" and surrendering your ALL to GOD then you still are in the hands of the enemy, to be used by him however he chooses. This of course, is something very few people seem to be aware of because if they were aware—there would be more people deciding to surrender their ALL over to CHRIST.

When your spirit is not of GOD and it is the enemy's, all the enemy wants is to destroy you. Although it does not seem possible, the enemy will have free access to your life to do his will and use your life for his evil plans. Many people have evil spirits who want them to be destroyed through: divorce; loss of income; loss of life, and cast into hell ultimately. The Bible gives an example of how spirits inside someone can lead them into life- and soul-threatening situations—like this young boy who was doing things he did not want to do:

Matthew 17:14-18 (KJV): 14And when they were come to the multitude, there came to him a certain man, kneeling down to him, and saying, 15LORD, have mercy on my son: for he is lunatic, and sore vexed: for oft times he falleth into the fire, and oft into the water. 1And I brought him to THY disciples, and they could not cure him. 17Then JESUS answered and said, O faithless and perverse generation, how long shall I be with you? How long shall I suffer you? Bring him hither to ME. 18And JESUS rebuked the devil; and he departed out of him: and the child was cured from that very hour.

Just like this scripture above describes the evil spirit and the devil ruling over the child causing him to fall into the fire and into the water, imagine that satan, who wants you to fail is actually trying to lead you to do the things that would destroy you and your eternal life—causing you to fall into the fire and into the water. Stop falling into the fires and deep waters the enemy wants to drag you in and out of. Be free of this evil—Surrender your ALL to CHRIST and choose GOD's Perfect Will over your own will.

2. HUMBLE HEARTS WILL WALK WITH THEIR GOD

(Words Received from Our LORD by Susan, June 22, 2013)

Susan, this is your GOD—I am ready to give you Words:

The hour is approaching of MY Return for the church. It closes in. Each day, I draw nearer. The Season is now! You are in the season to be watching closely. This is not the time to be sitting on your hands or closing your eyes. This is the time to be vigilant. Keep your nose pressed to the glass—watching, looking, listening for MY Trumpet Blast.

I will come like a thief in the night. If you are not watching, you will not be taken when I come back to rescue MY church, to bring out MY bride. She is gathering under MY Mantle: MY Blood Covering. I only have eyes for her—for MY bride: those who choose to follow ME, their GOD and to lay down their affection for the world and all it stands for.

MY bride has no taste for the world and its false attraction. Many have turned to the world for all their answers, hoping to receive truth for life's problems through men and MY enemy's works. He has always longed to lead men astray and only wants to deceive mankind and take MY children to hell. This is what happens, when MY children are asleep and not watching. They are deceived and easily fall into enemy hands.

Deception is running high now and the only way to discern Truth is by surrendering your life over to ME with a humble submission: pressing in to your GOD; receiving MY Blood Covering and Salvation that I earned for you by hanging on a cross with a brutal death. I willingly surrender MY ALL to die for you in your place, to cover your sins committed against a HOLY GOD, your FATHER, WHO has established Laws to live by.

Your sin is rebellion before your GOD, your CREATOR. All have sinned and fallen short of the Glory of GOD. Now, because of the awesome price I paid, I can buy back your Salvation: pay your penalty for your lifetime of sinful acts: treason against a HOLY GOD. Now, you can rest assured that your salvation is secured and you can spend eternity with your GOD instead of being cast away from MY Presence into eternal hell—punishment for your evil life.

Take freely MY Salvation and MY SPIRIT will come live in your spirit so that you can live sin-free by the Power of the HOLY SPIRIT, but you must first surrender your ALL. Give ME ALL of you and I will give you all of ME: MY Salvation and MY SPIRIT to reside within your heart to lead you, instruct you, comfort you, and assist you in life's difficult moments.

Come! Live life in all its fullness by the Power of MY HOLY SPIRIT. You decide: do you want to live your true destiny and the plan I have written for your life: MY Will for your life? Come into MY Saving Grace and Power to fight sin, expose evil, and bring you back to MY Kingdom on earth and in heaven. You will be ready to take flight when I come to retrieve MY bride.

Now is the time to make this exchange: your sin-filled life for MY Beautiful and perfect plans for you—plans I have penned long ago for you to walk in and live in peace to commune with your GOD and MAKER. Come get right with your GOD. Don't delay. Surrender your ALL.

Humble hearts will walk with their GOD. Only these will ever know ME, truly know ME. Humility is the narrow road. Come to MY Grace and Love everlasting.

I am the KING of kings

LORD of lords

HUMBLE GOD

Coordinating Scriptures:

1 Thessalonians 5:1-2 (KJV): 5But of the times and the seasons, brethren, ye have no need that I write unto you. 2 For yourselves know perfectly that the Day of the LORD so cometh as a thief in the night.

Matthew 24:31 (KJV): 31 And HE shall send HIS angels with a great sound of a trumpet, and they shall gather together HIS elect from the four winds, from one end of heaven to the other.

1 John 2:15 (KJV): Love not the world, neither the things that are in the world. If any man love the world, the love of the FATHER is not in him.

Jeremiah 29:11 (KJV): For I know the thoughts that I think toward you, saith the LORD, thoughts of peace, and not of evil, to give you an expected end.

Psalm 37:23 (KJV): The steps of a good man are ordered by the LORD: and HE delighteth in his way.

3. THIS IS THE HOUR OF REPENTANCE

Words of the LORD:

"This is the hour of repentance, weeping and wailing over your sinfulness."

(Words Received from Our LORD by Susan, June 23, 2013)

Susan, it is I, your GOD. I am ready to begin. These words are for whoever will listen and for whoever has a heart for their GOD:

Children of the MOST HIGH, I am asking you to repent before a HOLY GOD. This is the hour of repentance, weeping and wailing over your sinfulness, over your lust for the world, your lusting eyes for the world. You have put another god before ME, many gods, actually. You have placed ME at the bottom of your list. You have dishonored ME because you love the world more than ME. I am not at the top of the mind.

I am not the first thought in the morning or the last thought at night. Many of you spend very little time with ME throughout your days. You make lots of time for many other pursuits. You find many worldly activities more important than your pursuit of ME, your GOD. You make other people, other activities and other pursuits of greater worthiness to you than ME, your MAKER. Why do you think that is so?

You have clearly made up your mind to take the low road than to pursue the high road. The high road is a very narrow road. Very few will make their way to this very narrow road. The world will pull you away as you try to make your way down MY narrow road. The enemy will clutch and pull the people off the narrow road that leads to MY Salvation, MY Truth, and ultimately MY Kingdom where MY true followers come for eternity. You must set your sights on this narrow path. You must seek ME in all your ways. You must surrender your all to ME, your GOD, and I do mean your ALL.

I cannot accept a partial filling of your lamp oil: a partial relationship will not do. If you believe yourself ready to come with ME in MY Rapture, then you would have thrown off the world completely. You would have walked away from your own will, laid yourself before ME in repentance and begged to be in MY Perfect Will at all costs. Anything else puts you in danger of eternal failure: a failure to be saved and failing to be with GOD for eternity.

These words are sincere, they are serious. You must take them seriously if you want to be saved. Half-hearted love for GOD is as good as outright hatred of GOD. You either love ME, MY Will, and MY Ways or you reject ME. There is no middle ground.

Now decide for yourself: will you be with ME in My Kingdom for eternity or will you die in your sin apart from your GOD cast into eternal hell? Choices must be made—these are your choices to make: no one else's. Don't be deceived there is no other way. Come into MY Glorious Light, receive salvation, choose for ME, surrender your all to ME, repent of your ugly sin, and then come live in MY Will for your life.

These words are for your benefit. The time is short, come quickly and find your GOD. Cast your cares on ME. I will bear your burdens. I await your answer.

This is your GOD ALMIGHTY

The LOVER of your soul

Coordinating Scripture:

James 4:4 (KJV): Ye adulterers and adulteresses, know ye not that the friendship of the world is enmity with GOD? Whosoever therefore will be a friend of the world is the enemy of GOD.

Galatians 5:16-17 (KJV): 16This I say then, Walk in the SPIRIT, and ye shall not fulfil the lust of the flesh. 17For the flesh lusteth against the SPIRIT, and the SPIRIT against the flesh: and these are contrary the one to the other: so that ye cannot do the things that ye would.

Matthew 25:4 (KJV): 4 But the wise took oil in their vessels with their lamps.

Matthew 7:14 (KJV): Because strait is the gate, and narrow is the way, which leadeth unto life, and few there be that find it.

1 Peter 5:7 (KJV): Casting all your care upon HIM; for HE careth for you.

4. HOW TO HEAR THE VOICE OF GOD

End Times Prophecy Conference Presentation

"How to Hear the Voice of GOD" given by Donna McDonald:

June 8, 2013

My dear friends, my old friends and my new friends:

These words were dictated to me from the LORD. You see, I am not a public speaker, I am a servant. The LORD speaks and I am to obey. First of all I want to repent of my sins before a HOLY GOD, I cast out the enemy and send him to hell under the precious Name of YAHUSHUA, I cover this room, myself, and all the attendees with the precious blood of YAHUSHUA. I protect this area under the Holy Name of the LORD.

I pray to the LORD and I give HIM myself, I give HIM my arms, my legs, my body, my heart, my mind, my spirit. I give HIM everything. I tell HIM I want all of HIM and want to go deeper with HIM. Well, if you give HIM all of yourself and tell HIM you want more of HIM-all of HIM, something is going to happen. I received the gift of hearing

HIS Voice almost two years ago. HE has revealed amazing things to me ever since.

I want to tell you how I received this letter from the LORD. I was in the car with my kids in the back seat and my husband driving and we were going down the highway at 65 mph on the way to Florida. My son, Austin, set up my computer so it would act as a word processor. I said to the LORD that I was ready to hear a message from the HOLY SPIRIT about what I should say at the conference. HE spoke these words to me to share with you. I typed as I heard HIM speak. My family can attest to this. I read them the words as soon as I was finished typing them.

This is what HE wants to say to you. I have prayed and received these words and HE is speaking these words prophetically to you:

I created the stars in the sky and the sand on the beaches. I created birds and butterflies and leaves and trees. I have created mountains and oceans and lakes and paths and streams. I have created everything beautiful for you to enjoy. I created it all for you, MY children, to enjoy while you are firmly planted on this earth. I have also created the heavens for you to enjoy. All of you have had your feet firmly planted on this earth but not all of MY creation will see heaven.

They will stand at the gates of heaven and will meet ME Eye to eye some day, one day, but not all will hear, "Well done good and faithful servant." Only those who give ME their all will hear those Words. Only those who put aside ALL of their own hopes, plans, and dreams will ever see MY Home, the one MY FATHER created for ME and the one I have created for you. Only those children who place ME first in their lives will ever see ME Face to face and will enter heaven where I have created great places for you to enjoy.

23

It is not enough that you go to church, drive your mother to the store, read MY Bible occasionally or call out to ME in your time of need. No one's religion or their church traditions or their statues or idols ever saved them, nor their rote prayers. I want MY children to call out to ME everyday in prayer. I want MY children to look on ME as their BEST FRIEND, to treat ME like I am the BEST THING that ever happened to them. When I died on the cross, a horrible death, I became the BEST THING that ever happened to each one of you, I broke the curse once and for all over sin and over religion and all the do's and don'ts that the prior generation knew.

MY FATHER gave ME for you so that you would not have to suffer and endure the torture and pain that I did when I died for you on the cross: a feat that no man has ever endured and lived through like I did until I died late in the afternoon that day at Golgotha. I became the perfect sacrifice for you. I became your LAMB on that cold, cruel cross to suffer for you so that you would not have to. Why would MY children want to take 'matters,' in their own lives, into their own hands, instead of putting their lives into MY Capable GODLY Hands? Why would you think you know what is best for yourself when I know all and I have created all and I know the perfect plan for you?

Run from all evil. Run into MY Arms. The world that I created for you is dying and decaying little by little. It is a stench to MY FATHER. HE can hardly tolerate it anymore. HE is ready to take MY bride out and throw a big party for ME in Heaven. You are all invited. Just make sure you get there. You must "RSVP" by submitting your life and everything you love and enjoy and look forward to, to ME. Submit your ALL to ME.

I will tell you now, how you can hear MY Voice. You do not need to read a book, though you may want to. MY son, Dr. Virkler, has

24

written a book called "Dialogue with GOD" to assist you in hearing MY Voice. MY Words here are all you need. This is what you need to do:

1. Submit yourself to ME: your GOD. Live for ME. Do not plan ahead: just listen to ME and I will guide and direct your paths.

2. Quiet yourself and listen to what I have to say to you.

3. Focus on ME. Picture yourself sitting on a park bench or pleasant location looking at ME and conversing with ME. The picture MY daughter, Akiane, drew is the most correct picture of ME ever known on the earth. Look up MY picture on the internet so you will know WHO you are talking to.

4. Pray and ask for forgiveness of your sins before a HOLY GOD. Ask ME if there is anything I want to say to you. Then clear your mind and just listen for ME to speak.

5. I am a gentleman. I am a Patient and Humble GOD. I have needs and I have desires and I desire to be number ONE in your life. Most people do not think that I have needs, because I am their GOD, but I do have needs and I created you to meet MY needs.

6. I have a need for love and affection. I have a need to be given attention. I have a need for praise and worship and I have a need to hear YOUR VOICE. You want to hear MY VOICE: well, I want to hear YOUR VOICE as well.

When you submit to ME, quiet yourself, pray and repent and listen. You will hear MY Voice. I may not speak where you can listen right away, but I will eventually. Keep talking and listening and I will eventually respond to you. I respond verbally with a Still, Small Voice and also I respond by showing MYSELF to you. I show

MYSELF everytime you hear a baby cry, or see a majestic mountain, or a perfectly blue sky, a rainbow, a sunny sky peeking through the clouds, a field full of wildflowers or a doe and her fawn by the side of the road. I share these beautiful creations for all to see. No one can say they never knew there was a GOD. Even those deep in the rainforests of Africa can say they have seen their GOD in the beauty of created nature.

Pursue ME as your only hope, for I AM YOUR ONLY HOPE in this dark, dark world. Every moment the world is getting darker and is spiraling down. Only those who pursue ME one hundred percent and give ME their entire life and all their hopes, plans, and dreams will make it off this planet alive and well. Do not be those unwise children who choose darkness by not giving ME their one hundred percent. The world is getting more and more evil. The antichrist spirit is rising up as WE speak and breathe here. Choose for ME and Choose for Life: for I Am the WAY, the TRUTH, and the LIFE. No one comes to the FATHER except through ME.

The end, daughter: signed, sealed and delivered with a kiss.

Donna McDonald 5/21/13

The LORD's Words for Today

Dear Followers of CHRIST:

The Bible is full of scripture that speaks of perfection through CHRIST. Perfection with regards to CHRIST is also represented as "holiness," and "separation from the world." Perfection comes when someone is separated from the ways of the world—also known as holiness or leading a perfect life.

Many people say it is impossible to be perfect—who can be perfect? But the Bible has plenty to say about perfection and holiness:

Matthew 5:48: Be ye therefore perfect even as your FATHER is perfect...

Ephesians 5:27: that HE might present her to HIMSELF a glorious church, not having spot or wrinkle or any such thing, but that she should be holy and without blemish...

2 Corinthians 7:1 (KJV): Having therefore these promises, dearly beloved, let us cleanse ourselves from all filthiness of the flesh and spirit, perfecting holiness in the fear of GOD.

Hebrews 10:14 (KJV): For by one offering HE hath perfected for ever them that are sanctified.

2 Corinthians 7:1 (KJV): Having therefore these promises, dearly beloved, let us cleanse ourselves from all filthiness of the flesh and spirit, perfecting holiness in the fear of GOD.

1 Thessalonians 4:7 (KJV): For GOD hath not called us unto uncleanness, but unto holiness.

1 Peter 1:16 (KJV): Because it is written, Be ye holy; for I am holy.

To deny the concept of perfection and holiness for the individual in the Word of GOD, you would just about have to declare that the Holy Book and GOD are lying because it is written and there can be no denying it: GOD says, "Be Holy," meaning "Be perfect."

People say: "You can't be perfect, so why try?" Well that would be the best argument satan has for the people to give up on pursuing GOD and HIS Ways—can't be done, so why in the world would anyone even attempt it? So let's cling to our old ways and go after the world and the ways of the world. That holiness stuff is "pie in the sky" thinking… But CHRIST says in Luke 1:37 (KJV): For with GOD nothing shall be impossible and that is the key to our perfection and pursuit of holiness and/or separation to GOD. Here is how the individual pursues and comes to "perfection":

HOLY SPIRIT—HOLY SPIRIT—HOLY SPIRIT—HOLY SPIRIT
HOLY SPIRIT

The answer is by the Power of the HOLY SPIRIT within the fully-surrendered Christian (not the lukewarm, "half-full oil lamp" Christian) can the person pursue "perfection." There is NO other way. So if someone feels the standard of Biblical perfection is set too high and is completely unattainable, that would be because they have not made a FULL transfer of their sin-filled life with the perfection found by the Power of the HOLY SPIRIT working within the Christian who makes a full surrender to CHRIST.

5. YOUR BIBLE IS UNFOLDING BEFORE YOUR EYES

(Words Received from Our LORD by Susan, July 15, 2013)

Words from the LORD to Susan:

Susan it is I, your LORD. I want you to give MY children these words:

The hour closes in. MY children, you still do not want to pay attention. I have sent forth MY messengers, MY Words, MY Signs. I even forecasted what would happen many years ago. I gave this through MY Precious Word, through MY precious messengers, many years ago.

Today, those Words are as solid as they were many years ago. I, GOD, do not lie. What I say will happen is happening. Your Bible is unfolding before your eyes. Open up MY Word and it lines up with the times. Only those who are sleeping cannot see it. Only those who are willfully rebellious refuse to see the times they are living in. They do not want to believe that MY Words are coming to pass. They love this world too much and this interferes with their love of the world.

If you believe MY Words and follow MY Truth you would stop interacting with the world and you would sit up and pay attention to what is going on around you. As it is, you want to chase after everything that is revolting in this world. You lust after a world that has turned its back to ME. You have traded your soul with the devil and exchanged it for a brief walk with this evil world that is temporal and fading fast. Don't you know that if you pursue the wicked ways of this world you will only end up where the wicked are going?

Wake up MY children, wake up quickly. Stop prostituting yourself to an evil lover, who will take everything you have and leave you for destruction. These are not the Words of a harsh, unkind GOD. These are the Words of a Loving FATHER WHO is desperately trying to save HIS children who are about to fall over the edge of a cliff never to be recovered again.

You are turning right into the trap of the enemy. Your eyes are blinded to the Truth and the only way out is if you turn back to ME. You must come back to your GOD and make a humble surrender of your ENTIRE life. A portion of your life is not adequate. I want EVERYTHING or nothing at all. You either give ME everything or you will die by the sword: the sword of MY enemy who longs to put all of MY children in hell. And hell is broadening every day, accommodating all those children who are rejecting ME, their GOD.

If you are not fully and completely MINE, this message is for you. This is a warning and you now know what I require of you. You can never say that I have not warned you. I have warned you in many ways, so you will face ME without excuses on that day that we will be FACE-to-face. So when you stand in front of ME, will I embrace you as MY own or will I cast you out of MY Sight for eternity? This now, must be your choice, because I, GOD, cannot choose for you. I pray that you come with ME before it is too late.

This is your LORD and SAVIOR:

Great in Grace and Mercy;

Great in Justice and Truth

Coordinating Scripture:

Matthew 24:32-35 (KJV): 32 Now learn a parable of the fig tree; When his branch is yet tender, and putteth forth leaves, ye know that summer is nigh: 33 So likewise ye, when ye shall see all these things, know that it is near, even at the doors. 34 Verily I say unto you, This generation shall not pass, till all these things be fulfilled. 35 Heaven and earth shall pass away, but MY Words shall not pass away.

Isaiah 13:11 (KJV): And I will punish the world for their evil, and the wicked for their iniquity; and I will cause the arrogancy of the proud to cease, and will lay low the haughtiness of the terrible.

Revelation 6:8 (KJV): And I looked, and behold a pale horse: and his name that sat on him was Death, and Hell followed with him. And power was given unto them over the fourth part of the earth, to kill with sword, and with hunger, and with death, and with the beasts of the earth.

Romans 14:12 (KJV): So then every one of us shall give account of himself to GOD.

Isaiah 5:14 (KJV): Therefore hell hath enlarged herself, and opened her mouth without measure: and their glory, and their multitude, and their pomp, and he that rejoiceth, shall descend into it.

6. MY HEART ACHES OVER EVERY LOST SINNER WHO STEPS INTO ETERNITY APART FROM ME

(Words Received from Our LORD by Susan, July 7, 2013)

WE may begin:

This is your LORD and SAVIOR, YAHUSHUA:

I came that I might set the captives free—to deliver the lost...to bring Truth into the light. I have come so that mankind can grasp the Love of GOD. I wanted to show the affection of GOD through MY Salvation and MY Saving Grace.

I am a Loving GOD. MY Love is incomprehensible. I paid the penalty for MY lost race, Adam's race. I laid MYSELF low. I took the cursing, the scourging, the spittings. I took the bruising, the punishment. I bore the sins. I took the whippings. I laid low until I was empty. Even in the final moment, I suffered—it was sheer torture what I endured. All of MY Flesh was in pain. I ached and was in excruciating suffering right until I breathed MY Last. MY Heart was broken as I was betrayed by MY own people, the very ones I had spoken life into.

I saw the sufferings of mankind at the hand of MY enemy. If it were not for MY Willingness to endure the task of assuming the role of a human being and bearing the burdens of the sins of mankind on MY OWN Shoulders, all would be lost—burned up by the Wrath of GOD, ALMIGHTY GOD.

MY Crucifixion and Submission to be broken and suffer is your key to Salvation. It is your safe passage way. No other door or way will save men: lost men who have sinned beyond retribution. MY Blood given in exchange for the lost souls of men is sufficient to save the human race and to pull mankind out of the fire, everlasting hell fire. Yet hell broadens every day because men and their pride refuse to receive such a Great Salvation: that of GOD laying low, being beaten and abused beyond recognition for complete FULL payment for sin and evil. No other payment would have been so complete.

What do you say to this perfect deliverance? Will you receive it and surrender your ALL to ME, allow MY SPIRIT to have complete reign over your soul and life? This is what is expected of you to receive MY Salvation and Life-giving, Power-rendering SPIRIT, full time in your life to walk with you everywhere you go.

Don't be caught empty-handed without MY SPIRIT FULLY in your life when I Return for MY bride. You must hurry to come into this Loving Grace. Too many will keep their hands in their pockets refusing to lift hands in praise and surrender. Those with full pockets will be left behind. Is your pride too great for you to pull your hand from your pockets and to lift them upward in repentance and surrender?

You decide. What could be more important than the Salvation of your own soul?

Stop chasing the wind and this lost world. Let your will be done in your life. Step into a bright future away from soon-coming doom and destruction of an evil world. I will not wait forever on you to decide. Not much longer and I must deliver the church, MY Bride.

MY heart aches over every lost sinner who steps into eternity apart from ME, their GOD.

I AM that I AM

Eternal, Everlasting GOD

Coordinating Scripture:

Isaiah 61:1 (KJV): The SPIRIT of the LORD GOD is upon ME; because the LORD hath anointed ME to preach good tidings unto the meek; HE hath sent ME to bind up the brokenhearted, to proclaim liberty to the captives, and the opening of the prison to them that are bound;

Luke 4:17-21 (KJV): 17And there was delivered unto HIM the Book of the prophet Esaias. And when HE had opened the Book, HE found the place where it was written, 18The SPIRIT of the LORD is upon ME, because HE hath anointed ME to preach the gospel to the poor; HE hath sent ME to heal the brokenhearted, to preach deliverance to the captives, and recovering of sight to the blind, to set at liberty them that are bruised, 19To preach the acceptable year of the LORD. 20And HE closed the Book, and HE gave it again to the minister, and sat down. And the eyes of all them that were in the synagogue were fastened on HIM. 21And HE began to say unto them, This day is this Scripture fulfilled in your ears.

Mark 10:34 (KJV): And they shall mock HIM, and shall scourge HIM, and shall spit upon HIM, and shall kill HIM: and the third day HE shall rise again.

Isaiah 52:14 (KJV): As many were astonished at THEE; HIS Visage was so marred more than any man, and HIS form more than the sons of men:

7. RAPTURE DREAM

Tuesday 2 July 2013...........................

Dear Susan: I hope this finds you well. I just thought of sharing with you a rapture dream I experienced on Monday, 1 July 2013, in the very early hours of the day:

Here goes......................................

RAPTURE DREAM MONDAY, 1 JULY 2013

It was as if I was on a journey to go to my home town, so I thought; it was like some place I had been to before. As I travelled, I noticed that there were some clouds in the sky. As I looked in the sky to my left, I saw a red-like cloud in the form of a very big lion. At first I thought it would scare me, but I kept moving on. I looked the other direction (slightly to my right, in the sky) and saw some other clouds also shaped like a lion.

As I continued on my journey, I came to a certain homestead, where I wanted to ask for a short-cut to where I was going. There were two women at that homestead – one black, one white. The white woman was the first one to come and greet me. As she extended her hand to shake mine, the black woman suddenly intercepted the white woman, as if to stop her from greeting me. However, the white woman stood her ground and prevailed, and she then told me she was selling one of her cars. The black woman again wanted to stop the white woman from doing this, but the latter would not be deterred, and she went on ahead to show me the car. This she did after I had indicated in my mind that I could be interested in buying it.

Suddenly, as I was viewing the car, some events started happening around us. There was a lot of movement around us. I saw some 'floating chunks of green patches of land,' seemingly floating on some white, crispy clouds. I also saw what looked like some series of moving 'lights,' one after another (I also saw the same lights in my 11 April 2013 rapture dream). I also saw three moons in the sky and exclaimed to the women, "Hey, something is happening, do you see those three moons?" One of the women replied, "Oh, you only see three? There were 10 moons altogether!" Then I immediately remembered one of my past rapture dreams (27 May 2013, where I had dreamt about seeing 11 moons as one of the signs that had immediately preceded the rapture in that earlier dream). It then dawned on me that the rapture was actually about to happen.

I then knelt on the ground before GOD to thank HIM for HIS faithfulness in having given me a dream that had come true (the rapture about to happen). As I started praying in that kneeling position, I suddenly felt I was going to be raptured. Suddenly, feeling the Presence of GOD, I was 'sucked' up and went shooting into the atmosphere at a terrific speed. Like in my 11 April 2013 rapture dream, I could feel the wind blowing against my body and my face as I shot upwards. What was strange with this dream was that as I was shooting into the atmosphere, I could still feel that I was on my bed, as if the dream had turned into a vision. I hesitated going up a bit, and my speed began to slow down. As I yielded again to the force pulling me up, my speed of ascent started to increase again. I pulled back again, becoming afraid of the dark atmosphere, and I heard a voice saying, "Wait a minute." I opened my eyes and saw the darkness, and my fear, hesitation and resistance to go up finally caused the power taking me up to let go of me, and I came to fully on my bed at around 02:35am. At that time, my heart was racing, and I was enveloped in the Presence of GOD that I felt so intensely.

1 JOHN 3:2: "Beloved, now we are children of GOD; and it has not yet been revealed what we shall be, but we know that when HE is revealed, we shall be like HIM, for we shall see HIM as HE is," (NKJV).

"My Revelation Notes" from Susan:

The Bible speaks very clearly about living our lives apart from GOD's Will and that we need to be in GOD's Will everyday by surrendering ourselves to the LORD.

Today, people everywhere are disappointed with the outcome of their lives whether because they: are undergoing divorces; job failures; financial struggles; and on and on… But if only we would align ourselves with the Perfect Will of GOD, we would then be under the watchful eye and direction of GOD ALMIGHTY—GOD WHO knows the future, then WE CAN BE CONFIDENT in the direction we are moving in and not apart from GOD.

"My Revelation Notes" from Susan:

The LORD revealed to me about Satan saying: that he went wrong when he turned away from GOD to the creation to receive admiration from the creation and he became fully prideful which is the root of all evil. The LORD says that no one can be turning to and facing GOD all the time and remain prideful—you are only humble when you face GOD and humility is the root of all love.

8. YOU CHILDREN ARE OUT OF MY WILL IF YOU CANNOT SEE HOW DARK IT HAS BECOME

(Words Received from Our LORD by Susan, August 11, 2013)

LORD, what is it that you want me to do or say, I will listen.

I am ready to give you Words. I am ready to address these children once again.

I have come during this late hour to put forth this message. I want you to know that MY Coming is all so near, as you see the darkness growing, so also is MY Coming closing in. The two go hand in hand. This is how the bride knows that I am coming. She is sensitive to the growing darkness. Her spirit senses the growing darkness.

You children are out of MY Will if you cannot see how dark it has become. If the scales were off your eyes you could see it. Without MY SPIRIT in HIS Fullness these things are not easily seen. You must repent for your love for this world and the rejection of MY Truth—the Words of MY Book. The Words I spoke through the prophets of old with the signs I have given forth so very long ago that are even now coming to pass. I laid it out and nothing is amiss. Everything is happening, as I said it would.

I will come also as I said I would, but do not be dismayed, one will follow the other: as you see the signs coming to pass, so you will see ME breaking through the sky to collect MY bride. So as you see the signs coming together, so you will see ME Coming to rapture the church. One will follow the other. I am not a man that I should lie. MY Coming is close at hand, just as I said it would be. The Truth is in MY Book and I do not deviate from MY Truth.

Get ready, prepare. For whomsoever will receive this message: I will see MY Words to fruition.

This is the Great GOD of heaven and earth,

YAHUSHUA HA MASHIACH

Coordinating Scripture:

Amos 8:11 (KJV): Behold, the days come, saith the LORD GOD, that I will send a famine in the land, not a famine of bread, nor a thirst for water, but of hearing the words of the LORD.

Matthew 7:21 (KJV): Not everyone that saith unto ME, LORD, LORD, shall enter into the kingdom of heaven; but he that doeth the Will of MY FATHER which is in heaven.

Acts 9:17-18 (KJV): And Ananias went his way, and entered into the house; and putting his hands on him said, Brother Saul, the LORD, even JESUS, that appeared unto thee in the way as thou camest, hath sent me, that thou mightiest receive thy sight, and be filled with the HOLY SPIRIT. 18 And immediately there fell from his eyes as it had been scales: and he received sight forthwith, and arose, and was baptized.

Luke 21:11 (KJV): And great earthquakes shall be in diverse places, and famines, and pestilences; and fearful sights and great signs shall there be from heaven.

Matthew 24:32 (KJV): Now learn a parable of the fig tree; When his branch is yet tender, and putteth forth leaves, ye know that summer is nigh:

9. PARTIAL SURRENDER IS NO SURRENDER. I WILL NOT ACCEPT A LUKEWARM FAITH.

(Words Received from Our LORD by Susan, August 3, 2013)

I am ready to give you Words. Let us begin:

Children, dark clouds are rolling in. I am ready to descend and take MY bride home. She is lovely in all her ways. She follows her GOD. She does not look to the left or the right. She follows the straight and narrow path.

MY bride is focused on ME. She follows MY Truth and no other. She listens for MY Words in her spirit, because she has made a full surrender to ME. She has given ME her all and I AM her ALL-in-all.

She seeks ME all through the day. WE are not apart in OUR thoughts and views. MY Thoughts are hers. When I move, she moves. When I stop, she stops. She is MY Hands and Feet. MY Words come through her mouth to the people. She carries MY Gospel to those who are lost.

No one else carries the Truth, only MY bride: a unique people, separated unto ME, set apart from the world, who only have eyes for ME. These people, who are unique, are the ones I am coming back for: the few, the chosen, the ready—those who are sitting on the edge of their seats watching and waiting patiently for their GOD. These are the ones I died for. These are the ones I am coming to get.

Soon, very soon they will be going with ME as I pull them out to safety, out of a dark world that is crumbling under their feet. You can be part of MY bride, it is not too late. Just turn to ME, your GOD in FULL surrender. Lay your life down at MY Feet, give ME everything. I want it all.

Partial surrender is NO surrender. I will not accept a lukewarm faith. I will spew it out and leave you behind. Then you will see the error of your way as you will be left to face MY enemy and you have not seen yet the full magnitude of the aggression he has planned.

So come to ME now before it is too late. I… Your GOD IS waiting patiently for you, MY children. Turn to your CREATOR, the hour is short.

This is the MAKER of the heavens and the earth and the CREATOR of the future

I, GOD, have spoken

Coordinating Scripture:

Ephesians 5:21 (KJV): Submitting yourselves one to another in the fear of GOD.

Titus 2:14 (KJV): WHO gave HIMSELF for us, that HE might redeem us from all iniquity, and purify unto HIMSELF a peculiar people, zealous of good works.

1 Peter 2:9 (KJV): But ye are a chosen generation, a royal priesthood, an holy nation, a peculiar people; that ye should shew forth the praises of HIM WHO hath called you out of darkness into HIS Marvelous Light;

Revelation 3:16 (KJV): So then because thou art lukewarm, and neither cold nor hot, I will spue thee out of MY Mouth.

10. UNFORGIVENESS

The LORD's Words for Today (Posted at www.End-Times-Prophecy.Com)

Dear Followers of CHRIST:

In a previous Letter from the LORD, HE gave a warning to the people about "un-forgiveness" and the importance of forgiving everyone to be received into the Kingdom of GOD. A reader sent this powerful letter after reading the LORD's Letter on "un-forgiveness." I have decided to send his letter and to re-run the LORD's Letter about "un-forgiveness" along with it. Here is a letter from our reader, Evangelist Sommy Erekosima of Nigeria, who is graduate of Sonite Publishers Ltd, Publisher, End-Times Revelations Magazine and leader of GOD's Armour Bearers Outreach, a ministry that is engaged in witnessing CHRIST, organizing miracle crusades and training evangelists in Nigeria and abroad:

Bless you beloved Susan for delivering the LORD's un-diluted Truth. Several things happened that taught me the how to truly forgive and how to be delivered from un-forgiveness.

First, a Christian brother, who was highly gifted in prophesy and revelation died for four hours in 2003, 18th June. I had just concluded a three days waiting on the LORD without food and water.

This brother's anger and un-forgiving spirit was prayer number 11 on my prayer list. FATHER GOD heard my cry and gave him a second chance.

My Christian brother had a four hours after-death encounter. In his account he said, the Bible was opened before him and he was told that he could not enter heaven because of the spirit of un-forgiveneass. He said the angel told him that because I was pleading on his behalf, he has been granted a second chance to come back and make up. But he must not fail to alert the brethren that several Christians do not make heaven because of un-forgiveness.

Since then I have been preaching the sermon on Matthew 5:44 and it's amazing how many are in the trap of un-forgiveness.

Thank you for all your love for me and the household of CHRIST, our soon-coming GROOM.

Shalom,

Evangelist Sommy Erekosima, Nigeria

In a second note from Evangelist Sommy Erekosima, he wrote me (Susan), after I inquired if I could share his powerful story:

Beloved Susan, go ahead and share it. It's our little effort to rescue millions from falling into hell fire.

In fact, what I didn't add was that this Christian brother, who died and was refused entry into heaven had incredible gifts of prophesy and revelation. He used to follow me to crusades and then he could say many things GOD will do before time. One day, he commanded fire to come upon three robbers who attacked him on the road and they were slained.

Because of his gift he started to attract more prominence than myself - the crusade leader. But when he died, he said, I came face-to-face with the Mighty Book which was opened and the angel said, "You are not qualified to enter the gate of heaven." "But, because my servant (Sommy) is on his knees crying, you have been given a second chance."

"The angel told me to tell you (Sommy) to publish in your "End-Time Revelation Magazine" that the two common sins that affect Christians most are: 1.) Pride and 2.) Un-forgiveness. Tell the world that many great men of GOD that we suppose are in heaven, are not because of these two sins. I saw many of them crying when the Book was opened to show their record of un-forgiveness and pride," my brother in CHRIST said.

The truth is that I had a three days waiting alone with GOD on 15-17 June, 2003 in Abuja, Nigeria. During such meetings my phones, TV, and all communications were off. I ended up in the dry fast and the first phone call the following morning, 18th June was from my wife in Port Harcourt telling me that my friend and colleague was dead.

Meanwhile, my Christian brother was number 11 on my prayer list. All I was pleading for him during those three days was: "Oh LORD, deliver my brother from the spirit of anger." You can then understand why the news of his death troubled me, and I said to FATHER GOD, "How can you allow death to snatch my brother when I have been pleading on his behalf for the last three days?" GOD answered and raised my Christian brother up after four hours of having been confirmed dead.

So, I was not surprised when this friend and Christian brother said the LORD told him, "See my servant crying and pleading on your behalf and who was in Port Harcourt" and he didn't know I was waiting and could not have known that I was praying for him if not for the LORD having told him.

The LORD said to him: "For that reason you have a second chance, but let the world know of this!"

Susan, I believe it's the HOLY SPIRIT WHO wanted this truth published through you, because the "End-Time Revelation Magazine" which used to have a wide circulation in Nigeria that could have also published this testimony stopped circulation since 2001 because of lack of funds arising from gross embezzlement from the retailers who were mainly church ushers.

But GOD, WHO CANNOT BE LIMITED, may have decided to use your platform to publish it.

Let the NAME of our Awesome GOD be glorified!

Evangelist Sommy Erekosima, Nigeria

Words of the LORD:

"I am your GOD and I am telling you, that you will not enter MY Kingdom if you have un-forgiveness for anyone."

(Words Received from Our LORD by Susan, July 21, 2013)

I am ready to begin: Children, this is your GOD speaking. I am going to speak on the topic of forgiveness.

MY children, you are unforgiving. You hold onto un-forgiveness like it is a prize cow. I am your GOD and I am telling you, that you will not enter MY Kingdom if you have un-forgiveness for anyone. This cannot be. I will not tolerate an unforgiving heart. It is an abomination to ME. You must forgive and forget and let go of those past sadness's.

I will release you from your hurt and pain, if you just turn to ME. I am the ONE WHO will bring you healing: the heart healing that you need so badly. I will mend your broken hearts. I will deliver you from heartache. I can do it, no one else. Other people will disappoint you. They do not have the heart of GOD. Their hearts are imperfect and human. They lack sensitivity and grace. I am the HEART that beats for eternity. MY Heart is strong and vibrant, resilient, and ever-beating.

Lay your sadness's down at MY Feet: all the death blows that are dealt by MY enemy, who works through those around you. Forgive those around you for the way the enemy has worked through them to cause you pain. Although you suffer, it is at the hand of the enemy more than those around you. They are just weak, because they do not have the Power of MY HOLY SPIRIT to ward off sin and walk perfect in MY Will.

It is only by the Power of MY HOLY SPIRIT that anyone can do MY Will. You must surrender your ALL to ME to be in MY Will, to have the Power of MY HOLY SPIRIT to ward off evil. To be made ready to come into MY Kingdom you must be in MY Perfect Will.

Ask ME to be in MY Will. I will lead you down paths of righteousness. I will make you ready for MY Coming. There is no other way. I will give you the spotless garments that are required to stand in MY presence, just ask ME and do not delay. The hour of MY Return is swiftly moving in. I do not want to leave you behind to face the terror of MY enemy.

Your GOD has Spoken

Do not delay in preparing for MY Coming

Coordinating Scripture:

Matthew 6:15 (KJV): But if ye forgive not men their trespasses, neither will your FATHER forgive your trespasses.

Ephesians 6:12 (KJV): For we wrestle not against flesh and blood, but against principalities, against powers, against the rulers of the darkness of this world, against spiritual wickedness in high places.

Psalm 23:3 (KJV): HE restoreth my soul: HE leadeth me in the paths of righteousness for HIS Name's sake.

Galatians 6:8 (KJV): For he that soweth to his flesh shall of the flesh reap corruption; but he that soweth to the SPIRIT shall of the SPIRIT reap life everlasting.

Galatians 5:24 (KJV): And they that are CHRIST's have crucified the flesh with the affections and lusts.

11. READ MY WORD AS IF IT IS THE LAST BOOK ON EARTH

(Words Received from Our LORD by Susan, September 1, 2013)

I will give you Words for the people.

There are drumbeats beating in the distance. It is the sound of the hoof beats of MY horse and the horses of MY angels coming to get MY bride. Do you hear it, MY children? Do you hear the beating of their feet on the ground? Do you hear the noise of the rumblings in the atmosphere? Do you feel the earth shaking under your feet? Do you hear the tremor of the hearts beating of the people at the sight of what is happening all over the earth as they witness a new age coming about—the dawning of the last days?

MY enemy is about to be exposed. Soon, the world will know the Truth, but it will be too late for those left behind. That is the reality that is about to set in. The true evil is about to be unveiled. The tarp is about to be pulled away from the master plan of the enemy to steal; kill and destroy mankind.

Children, if you are not in the Will of the FATHER when I come back to claim MY bride, you will be left behind to face the worst. MY enemy will mark you, kill you, and destroy you and if you refuse this mark you will die a gruesome death or worse, you will meet death in sudden destruction and be sent to hell apart from MY Salvation at the point the church is raptured.

Is this clear enough for you? You must get right with your GOD. Kneel before MY Holiness, surrender your ALL to ME, place your life at MY Feet, make a sincere repentance to ME of your sin, turn to forgive all others, and request for MY SPIRIT to fill you, to lead you, and to guide you into all Truth.

Read MY Word as if it is the last book on earth. Knowledge of GOD is power: power over sin; power over death; power over life; and power over Love Everlasting in the Kingdom of GOD. There is no place else to turn for the Truth but to ME and MY Word. Everything else is false and deceiving.

You have been warned over and over, yet few are following ME in the Way I desire. Many have allowed this world to be their god. So soon, the god of this world will take over those who want him more than ME. I am giving you these last warnings because MY Love for you is Great and because I know what lies ahead. You can never come to ME and say that I did not warn you.

Make preparations now.

This is your GOD

HOLY ONE from Above

Coordinating Scripture:

John 10:10 (KJV): The thief cometh not, but for to steal, and to kill, and to destroy: I am come that they might have life, and that they might have it more abundantly.

Revelation 13:17 (KJV): And that no man might buy or sell, save he that had the mark, or the name of the beast, or the number of his name.

Daniel 7:25 (KJV): And he shall speak great words against the MOST HIGH, and shall wear out the saints of the MOST HIGH, and think to change times and laws: and they shall be given into his hand until a time and times and the dividing of time.

1 Thessalonians 5:3 (KJV): For when they shall say, Peace and safety; then sudden destruction cometh upon them, as travail upon a woman with child; and they shall not escape.

Job 21:14 (KJV): Therefore they say unto GOD, Depart from us; for we desire not the knowledge of THY Ways.

Hosea 4:6 (KJV): MY people are destroyed for lack of knowledge: because thou hast rejected knowledge, I will also reject thee, that thou shalt be no priest to me: seeing thou hast forgotten the law of thy GOD, I will also forget thy children.

2 Peter 1:3 (KJV): According as HIS Divine Power hath given unto us all things that pertain unto life and godliness, through the knowledge of HIM that hath called us to glory and virtue:

12. WEANING CHRISTIANS OFF HALLOWEEN

Dear Followers of CHRIST: This Special Edition Letter: "Weaning Christians Off Halloween" features Words from the LORD GOD about Halloween (see two letters below) and introducing the new Facebook page and campaign "Weaning Christians Off Halloween." One definition of the word "wean" is:

stop somebody from having something: to cause somebody to go without something that has become a habit or that is much liked

And that is precisely what we are trying to do—educate and communicate to Christians the problem with embracing a holiday that represents evil and is the enemy of the church. We will be posting a flood of information about Halloween and the deceptions the Christians have fallen into through the culture/times around them to embrace evil.

Please visit the FB and see regular updates with important information to educate about the deception in the culture to deceive the Christians:

https://www.facebook.com/pages/Weaning-Christians-Off-Halloween/604312249611699

ANNOUNCING: Our New FACEBOOK Page: END TIMES CHURCHES:

Many Christians want to know why churches are NOT talking about end times when it is so blatantly obvious that we are in the end times--SO this page was started for churches to promote themselves if they proudly preach that LORD JESUS is returning for HIS bride--HIS church in the coming rapture. If you preach baptism of the HOLY SPIRIT--please let the people know and take the mystery out of their frustration of finding churches that preach the TRUTH and the HEART OF GOD. If your church is NOT PREACHING END TIMES AND HOLY SPIRIT BAPTISM--YOU ARE NOT IN THE WILL OF THE FATHER.

https://www.facebook.com/locatingendtimeschurches

13. THERE IS A DARKNESS ON THIS EARTH THAT IS SPREADING LIKE A WILDFIRE

(Words Received from Our LORD by Donna McDonald, September 8, 2013)

Daughter, I have a Word, a letter for you on Halloween. Take it down.

Daughter you must get this out to the people. It is vital for their health, vitality and salvation. Children, this is your LORD speaking, YAHUSHUA. I am your GOD and I am dictating this letter to this daughter for your benefit.

There is a darkness on this earth that is spreading like a wildfire. The wildfire is from the enemy. He is attempting to spread hell to the earth. He wants to engulf the earth in flames and take it over for himself. I will not let him. But he will take many captive and prisoner to his deep, dark dungeon called hell.

The people will be led astray and many will not know what hit them until they land in the deep, dark pit called hell. I want to inform you there is another way. Children, the darkness over the earth is highlighted by a holiday that the enemy calls "Halloween." Halloween is the holiday that takes place a day, a night before All Saints Day. This day was set apart for ME and what is "Holy" but the evil one in trying to mock ME and copy ME as he knows best to do.

He concocted a holiday to worship himself. It is called "Halloween." It is NOT a harmless and fun day for the children. Instead it is a day that is dedicated to the dead, the evil, and the corrupt. More satanic rituals occur on this day than on all the other days of the year put together. The evil one brings his evil and the people dedicated to evil out in full force. More animal sacrifices and human sacrifices occur on this day than on any other day of the year.

Now, do you believe this is a harmless holiday for the children? Would you want your children to dress up and ask for a 'trick or treat' knowing that this day brings animal and human sacrifices? What if the animal or human sacrificed was your child or loved one? What would you think of the day then? Children, you must put down all references to this day, all talk of it unless to warn and educate the others on its evil.

You must NOT go out and celebrate in any way, shape, or form on this day or night lest you come in contact with evil. It is best to stay at home and cook a home-cooked meal and read your Bible as a family. That way you are not out in the world on this evil night called Halloween. Do you understand ME? If not, what part of this do you not understand? If you can read this then you can understand this. There might be those of you who do not believe this and to those I say, "Hallelujah." Hallelujah is a word to praise your LORD. If you do not understand then praise ME anyway and I will bring the Truth to you in a manner and way you can understand to get the message across. I will educate you and enlighten you to the Truth of the day called "Halloween." You must first want the Truth and everything else will be added unto you.

Blessings from on High:

Your FATHER, YAHUSHUA HA'MASHIACH, Amen, Amen, Amen

Words of the LORD:

"Everything that circulates around this evil day glorifies MY enemy."

(Words Received from Our LORD by Susan Davis, September 6, 2013)

This is a letter for MY children. These days are dark and MY children have turned against their GOD. They are rabble-rousers. They want to cause ME trouble and make trouble. I am sullen at the darkness all around. The darkness closes in all over the earth. MY children embrace evil like it is a dearly beloved baby blanket. They are running to and fro to grasp evil. There is so much evil on earth that the people are completely dumbed-down to what they are doing and how they have come to be so far from their GOD.

I want to address this matter of the dark holiday approaching. It is a day that is meant to glorify MY enemy. Everything that circulates around this evil day glorifies MY enemy. It puts him at the center of the hearts of MY children, who, I, GOD, created. Their focus is on him and the love of his ways. I am so sickened of this I could puke.

MY children have slipped so far from ME. They cannot see the dark tunnel they are digging for themselves. They are taking shovels and digging themselves a gateway to hell and MY enemy is standing by assisting them.

Children, you must awaken to this Truth. Stop embracing this evil, let go of and quit handling this evil. Each day that you focus on MY enemy, you are one day closer to hell. MY coming is nigh, and although I know the day and the hour, you must prepare because of this day you know not. I will come as a thief in the night and only those prepared will be coming with ME. All those left behind will then live with this evil tyrant in full force. This day approaches: be not weary of preparing for MY coming. Only those who are ready are going with ME.

This is your LORD GOD

GREAT and MIGHTY

STRONG in TRUTH

PURVEYOR of LIGHT

14. I LOVE LIKE NO OTHER

Dear Followers of CHRIST: Thank you for your continued support of the LORD's End Time Prophecy ministry. Please note that our website is under major reconstruction and we hope to come back even better than ever. As soon as the site is up and running again we will notify you—in the meantime, here are important words from the LORD and some other important messages below them. GOD bless, Susan

Words of the LORD:

"I Love Like NO Other..."

(Words Received from Our LORD by Susan Davis, September 29, 2013)

I have a Word for the children:

Children of MINE: this is your GOD. Soon I will bring devastation to the world after I have removed MY cherished ones. I will allow the world to experience the result of its rejection of ME, it's GOD, CREATOR.

The world will come completely unhinged. It will fall into disarray, as it has never before and as it never will again. All this is before you—coming at lightning speed. Dark clouds are looming on all four corners of the globe to envelope this world that has turned its back to ME, rejected ME. All four corners have rejected its GOD.

Where will you go for peace? Where will you turn? The world cannot be trusted. You are out of options. Turn to ME, your GOD, your SAVIOR. I am the ONE: the Only ONE WHO can save you now. Don't delay in turning back to ME. Put out your hand—surrender to MY Will. Give ME your ALL: your heart; your soul; your mind; your love.

I am calling out to you—don't lose your way, your eternal way. Come seek the only love that is consistent... reliable... everlasting...unchanging... never-failing... all-consuming. Come seek ME with reckless abandon, as I already have when I put MY Life on the cross: I died with passion and an ALL-CONSUMING LOVE for you.

I love like NO OTHER! Don't reject this love for a weak alternative. I am the LOVER of your soul, but if you choose MY enemy and the world to give your heart away to, I will allow you to have your way.

MY Love calls for a complete surrender—you must choose ALL of ME or none of ME—there is no alternative. Your INCOMPLETE relationship with ME is the same as NO relationship. I will spit you out. MY Words are true!

Who are you for: ME, your GOD or the enemy of your soul? You may choose. You have this choice to make. Very few choose their GOD. Very few will be removed to safety when I come for MY own.

I am giving you these warnings even as darkness is closing in around you. Choose wisely.

This is your LORD—SAVIOR over ALL

Coordinating Scripture:

Matthew 24:21 (KJV):For then shall be great tribulation, such as was not since the beginning of the world to this time, no, nor ever shall be.

Mark 12:28-30 (KJV): 28 And one of the scribes came, and having heard them reasoning together, and perceiving that he had answered them well, asked him, Which is the first commandment of all? 29 And JESUS answered him, The first of all the commandments is, Hear, O Israel; The LORD our GOD is one LORD: 30 And thou shalt love the LORD thy GOD with all thy heart, and with all thy soul, and with all thy mind, and with all thy strength: this is the first commandment.

Revelation 3:16 (KJV): So then because thou art lukewarm, and neither cold nor hot, I will spue thee out of my mouth.

Matthew 24:37 (KJV): But as the days of Noah were, so shall also the coming of the SON of man be.

Joel 2:1-2 (KJV): Blow ye the trumpet in Zion, and sound an alarm in my holy mountain: let all the inhabitants of the land tremble: for the day of the LORD cometh, for it is nigh at hand; 2 A day of darkness and of gloominess, a day of clouds and of thick darkness, as the morning spread upon the mountains: a great people and a strong; there hath not been ever the like, neither shall be any more after it, even to the years of many generations.

15. I WILL NOT BE ABLE TO REMOVE YOU WITH AND AS MY BRIDE IF YOU ARE MARRIED TO ANOTHER

(Words Received from Our LORD by Susan Davis, October 1, 2013)

Let ME give you Words:

I am a GOD of Great Proportions. I am from eternal to eternal. MY BEING cannot be comprehended. I am from beginning to end—the ALPHA and OMEGA.

I am ready to take MY Place in the Heavens as your Great MASTER to you, MY bride; to bring you into MY Heavenlies. I am looking forward to the moment when our eyes will meet and you MY lovely bride will see ME FACE–to-face. This is the moment I long for and it is closer to you than it is far off.

I have place ready for you, MY bride. I have many rooms prepared. MY FATHER has made a beautiful home for you: it is nothing like the homes on earth. There is a place waiting where there are no tears, there is no pain—only rest for MY children: peace and comfort. It is an eternal gift from your FATHER Above.

This awaits you, MY bride: beauty unspeakable—nothing on earth compares. There is nothing to compare it to. No one can even imagine the things I have prepared for those who love ME.

You must "KNOW" ME. You must choose to be INTIMATE with ME. This is not possible if you engage with every other idol that comes across your doorstep. An idol can be anything that takes your love away from ME—anything that has taken MY Place in your heart is an idol. I will not be able to remove you WITH and AS MY bride if you are married to another. Your heart must be singularly focused on ME or you are outside MY Will and you will be outside MY Kingdom.

Examine your heart. What takes precedence over ME, your MAKER, CREATOR? What do you spend more time with than ME? What consumes you more than your love for ME?

Does it seem I am jealous? I am a Jealous GOD!

I Created you.

I Gave you life.

I Gave you breath.

I am Jealous-hearted over you—but if you choose against ME, I will allow this choice and your choice will put you in the will of the devil and you will be for him and remain with him to end up in the pits of hell where there is torment and torture and the worm never dies.

Please reconsider your position against ME! What idol is worth your destruction? Come back to your First LOVE—your GOD Eternal. You have a short amount of time remaining as the world grows darker each day. Please heed MY Cries. I Cry out for you. O' MY lost children, please turn back to ME, your GOD, your MAKER. MY Heart is weeping over you...Turn! Turn! Turn!

Coordinating Scripture:

1 Corinthians 13:12 (KJV): For now we see through a glass, darkly; but then FACE to face: now I know in part; but then shall I know even as also I am known.

Revelation 22:13 (KJV): I am ALPHA and OMEGA, the BEGINNING and the END, the FIRST and the LAST.

Revelation 21:4 (KJV): And GOD shall wipe away all tears from their eyes; and there shall be no more death, neither sorrow, nor crying, neither shall there be any more pain: for the former things are passed away.

1 Corinthians 2:9 (KJV): But as it is written, Eye hath not seen, nor ear heard, neither have entered into the heart of man, the things which GOD hath prepared for them that love HIM.

Exodus 34:14 (KJV): For thou shalt worship no other god: for the LORD, WHOSE Name is JEALOUS, is a Jealous GOD:

Deuteronomy 30:15 (KJV): See, I have set before thee this day life and good, and death and evil;

16. FEAR OF GOD

Dear Followers of CHRIST:

Today—I want to talk about the BEGINNING of understanding of the LORD: Fear of GOD. Today's Christians talk a lot about GOD's grace to the point that the "Fear of GOD" is almost ham strung. Why should anyone fear GOD when there is grace?

Well GOD IS FULL of grace, but people have lost sight of the "Fear of GOD." How do I know this? Because of the vast number in the church who are lukewarm. You can't truly fear GOD and remain lukewarm. It is the understanding of the fear of GOD that will drive you right out of the lukewarm state.

If you read the Bible, you will find several people who were lukewarm or worse: completely cold toward GOD, who lacked the understanding of fearing GOD that clearly led to bad outcomes: lessons that the lukewarm church is not embracing because they are disregarding this part of the Bible and this side of GOD. For example:

Nebuchadnezzar lifted himself up in his heart above GOD and while the words were still in his mouth GOD brought him down: Daniel 4:30-32 (KJV): 30The king spake, and said, Is not this great Babylon, that I have built for the house of the kingdom by the might of my power, and for the honour of my majesty? 31While the word was in the king's mouth, there fell a Voice from heaven, saying, O king Nebuchadnezzar, to thee it is spoken; The kingdom is departed from thee. 32 And they shall drive thee from men, and thy dwelling shall be with the beasts of the field: they shall make thee to eat grass as oxen, and seven times shall pass over thee, until thou know that the most High ruleth in the kingdom of men, and giveth it to whomsoever he will.

Aaron's sons were disobedient to GOD and Aaron's status as High Priest could not even save them: Leviticus 10:1-2 (KJV): And Nadab and Abihu, the sons of Aaron, took either of them his censer, and put fire therein, and put incense thereon, and offered strange fire before the LORD, which he commanded them not. 2And there went out fire from the LORD, and devoured them, and they died before the LORD.

Korah challenged GOD's choice of leadership in Moses and Aaron and he was destroyed by GOD: Numbers 16:3-4 (KJV): 3And they gathered themselves together against Moses and against Aaron, and said unto them, Ye take too much upon you, seeing all the congregation are holy, every one of them, and the LORD is among them: wherefore then lift ye up yourselves above the congregation of the LORD? 4And when Moses heard it, he fell upon his face:

Numbers 16:31-33 (KJV): 31And it came to pass, as he had made an end of speaking all these words, that the ground clave asunder that was under them: 32And the earth opened her mouth, and swallowed them up, and their houses, and all the men that appertained unto Korah, and all their goods. 33They, and all that appertained to them, went down alive into the pit, and the earth closed upon them: and they perished from among the congregation.

 This is not restricted to Old Testament teaching—let's also look into the New Testament for example:

 Herod allowed the people to praise him as if he were GOD and GOD destroyed him: Acts 12:21-23 (KJV): 21And upon a set day Herod, arrayed in royal apparel, sat upon his throne, and made an oration unto them. 22And the people gave a shout, saying, It is the voice of a god, and not of a man.23And immediately the angel of the LORD smote him, because he gave not GOD the glory: and he was eaten of worms, and gave up the ghost.

Ananias and Sapphira deliberately lied and stole from GOD and they too were immediately destroyed by their actions: Acts 5:1-11 (KJV): But a certain man named Ananias, with Sapphira his wife, sold a possession, 2 And kept back part of the price, his wife also being privy to it, and brought a certain part, and laid it at the apostles' feet. 3 But Peter said, Ananias, why hath Satan filled thine heart to lie to the HOLY GHOST, and to keep back part of the price of the land? 4Whiles it remained, was it not thine own? And after it was sold, was it not in thine own power? Why hast thou conceived this thing in thine heart? Thou hast not lied unto men, but unto GOD. 5 And Ananias hearing these words fell down, and gave up the ghost: and great fear came on all them that heard these things. 6 And the young men arose, wound him up, and carried him out, and buried him. 7 And it was about the space of three hours after, when his wife, not knowing what was done, came in. 8 And Peter answered unto her, Tell me whether ye sold the land for so much? And she said, Yea, for so much. 9 Then Peter said unto her, How is it that ye have agreed together to tempt the SPIRIT of the LORD? Behold, the feet of them which have buried thy husband are at the door, and shall carry thee out. 10 Then fell she down straightway at his feet, and yielded up the ghost: and the young men came in, and found her dead, and, carrying her forth, buried her by her husband. 11 And great fear came upon all the church, and upon as many as heard these things.

Make the "Fear of GOD" your priority because the Bible says the Fear of GOD is the BEGINNING of understanding. This should be the FIRST thing you understand about GOD—to fear HIM. Understanding that even CHRIST said to Satan: Thou shalt not tempt the LORD thy GOD. Even CHRIST understood and respected WHO GOD HIS FATHER was and that GOD was to be feared, respected, and revered. Too many today have absolutely NO respect for GOD, WHO HE is, and what HE stands for, and ultimately what HE is capable of.

Matthew 4:5-7 (KJV): 5 Then the devil taketh HIM up into the holy city, and setteth HIM on a pinnacle of the temple, 6 And saith unto HIM, If THOU be the SON of GOD, cast THYSELF down: for it is written, HE shall give angels charge concerning thee: and in their hands they shall bear thee up, lest at any time thou dash thy foot against a stone. 7 JESUS said unto him, It is written again, Thou shalt not tempt the LORD thy GOD.

1 Samuel 12:24 (KJV): Only fear the LORD, and serve HIM in truth with all your heart: for consider how great things HE hath done for you.

Psalm 2:11 (KJV): Serve the LORD with fear, and rejoice with trembling.

Psalm 19:9 (KJV): The fear of the LORD is clean, enduring for ever: the judgments of the LORD are true and righteous altogether.

Psalm 25:14 (KJV): The secret of the LORD is with them that fear HIM; and HE will shew them HIS Covenant.

Proverbs 9:10 (KJV): The fear of the LORD is the beginning of wisdom: and the knowledge of the holy is understanding.

17. I AM THE GOD OF SECOND CHANCES, BUT TIME IS RUNNING OUT...

(Words Received from Our LORD by Susan, October 29, 2013)

Children, it is I, your LORD.

You believe I am never coming back. You say this to each other, "HE says HE's coming, but HE doesn't come!"

MY children, this is your GOD speaking: Listen closely: I AM COMING! No, you will not know the day or the hour, but you can know the season and this is the season. The signs are appearing and you cannot deny MY coming is near.

I have given you many markings to follow. MY signs have been clear and they are coming to pass. Only those who don't want to follow ME are not seeing it. They do not want to know because they do not want to know ME, their GOD. Those who follow ME closely can see what is happening around them. They can see the darkness moving in, darker than it has ever been.

This is not the time to be sleeping at the wheel. This is not the time to be ignoring your GOD. If you keep sleeping you are going to miss MY Coming. Will I find any with faith when I return? Many and most are disloyal to their GOD. Very few are looking forward to MY Coming. Wake up and pay attention! Come out of your spiritual slumber! Open your spiritual eyes and see the darkness around you! Stop letting the things of the world move you to distraction! Take your hands off the world! Come wash your hands and your garments in MY Blood. Come wash them in MY Word. Make ready for MY coming.

Warn your neighbors and your friends. You will have blood on your hands if you don't warn the people around you. Who else can I send if not MY chosen bride? Only she has the truth and the map to the narrow path. All others are lost and misled: blind leading the blind.

Strike a match, start a fire, let MY HOLY SPIRIT Wind blow on the fire. Let the Truth blaze like a fire from your heart through your hands, through your mouth, through your feet. Let the world see the fire of MY True Gospel through MY people, MY bride. You are the only ones who have the Truth. You must not hide a Light under a bushel basket!

I want you to stop being comfortable in this world. I want you to be uncomfortable at the sight of the lost all around you. I want you to stop being comfortable in this world: you are just passing through.

You are a foreigner in this land. You must be like soldiers going to war. Many lives are at stake. This is their only chance. If they fail this test, they will be lost forever. Wake up church, get busy! Don't waste another moment...so many will be lost for eternity...so many are already lost.

If you come with ME, I will open many doors. Just open your mouth. I will put the words in your mouth. I will bring the people to your doorstep for you to talk to about MY Gospel. Once I take MY bride from the earth, the enemy will move in and the people will have a much harder time getting to MY Salvation. It will not be easy for MY "left behind" church. They will have to die at the hand of MY enemy to make it into MY Kingdom. So do not let these golden moments slip by you. These are precious, golden moments.

I am the GOD of Second Chances, but time is running out...

Coordinating Scriptures:

2 Peter 3:4 (KJV): And saying, Where is the promise of HIS coming? For since the fathers fell asleep, all things continue as they were from the beginning of the creation.

Mark 13:28 (KJV): Now learn a parable of the fig tree; When her branch is yet tender, and putteth forth leaves, ye know that summer is near:

Luke 18:8 (KJV): I tell you that HE will avenge them speedily. Nevertheless when the SON of man cometh, shall HE find faith on the earth?

Job 41:19 (KJV): Out of HIS Mouth go burning lamps, and sparks of fire leap out.

Psalm 119:105 (KJV): THY Word is a lamp unto my feet, and a light unto my path.

Proverbs 6:23 (KJV): For the commandment is a lamp; and the law is light; and reproofs of instruction are the way of life:

Matthew 25:3 (KJV): They that were foolish took their lamps, and took no oil with them:

Luke 11:33 (KJV): No man, when he hath lighted a candle, putteth it in a secret place, neither under a bushel, but on a candlestick, that they which come in may see the light.

18. WHY DO YOU THINK I HAVE NO SAY OVER THIS WORLD?

(Words Received from Our LORD by Susan, October 28, 2013)

This is the Word of the LORD.

Today I am about to give you the Word that lays heavy on MY Heart toward My people, even those who use MY Name and say I Am their GOD.

I am very dissatisfied by MY children and their pursuit of the world. I Am the GOD that created everything. I spoke it all into existence. I spoke and it all came to life. I sustain everything. I, and, I alone.

Nothing exists without ME. There is nothing that can be considered living except I made it possible. I am the Great "I AM." I live and breathe, I exist. I was before the mountains, before the stars. I am the Great and Powerful GOD. You would not breathe without ME. I am in charge of whether you live or breathe. This is MINE to do.

Why do you think I have no say over this world? If you believed I was in control you would stop chasing the world for all your answers, to give your love to, to pay homage to. If you believed that I am in control, you would stop pursuing other wooden idols, giving all your time to that which looks better to you than your GOD. I am low on your rung of priorities.

Listen to ME: if you don't stop pursuing the world as your "only lover," I am going to release MY Hand of protection over you. As it is, you may already have walked away from MY Protecting, Guiding Hand. To turn back to the world is a very grievous matter, after touching and handling the things of GOD. If you are sitting on the fence between ME and the world, you have already chosen against ME. I cannot call you, "MINE" if your love for ME is half-way and limited to brief moments of your time. At the point we meet I will declare, "I never knew you," and you will be cast away from ME as a foul stench and a worker of iniquity.

Wake up O' walking dead church of the lukewarm. I will leave you behind when I come for MY glorious church. MY bride who follows MY will is surrendered fully to MY Will. MY bride has discarded her pursuit of the world for something better: to follow her LORD, SAVIOR, and MASTER.

This is MY bride, MY True Church. This is who I Am coming back soon to get, very soon. Wake up, dead church! You have precious little time to meet and know your GOD—to become stain-free, and ready to enter MY Kingdom by the Power of MY HOLY SPIRIT. Seek ME. Lay your life down before ME. Give ME a FULL surrender. Let go of the world and all she stands for. WHO are you for? ME: the GOD of the living, breathing, or MY enemy, leader of the dead and dying? Pursue GOD! Find life!

I AM Has Spoken

Coordinating Scripture:

Genesis 2:7 (KJV): And the LORD GOD formed man of the dust of the ground, and breathed into his nostrils the breath of life; and man became a living soul.

Luke 13:23-27 (KJV): Then said one unto HIM, LORD, are there few that be saved? And HE said unto them, 24 Strive to enter in at the strait gate: for many, I say unto you, will seek to enter in, and shall not be able. 25 When once the MASTER of the house is risen up, and hath shut to the door, and ye begin to stand without, and to knock at the door, saying, LORD, LORD, open unto us; and HE shall answer and say unto you, I know you not whence ye are: 26 Then shall ye begin to say, We have eaten and drunk in THY Presence, and THOU hast taught in our streets. 27 But HE shall say, I tell you, I know you not whence ye are; depart from ME, all ye workers of iniquity.

Acts 7:51 (KJV): Ye stiff-necked and uncircumcised in heart and ears, ye do always resist the HOLY GHOST: as your fathers did, so do ye.

19. DON'T THINK IT STRANGE IF PEOPLE ARE "OFFENDED"

Dear Followers of CHRIST: If you are warning people of CHRIST's soon-coming and the Gospel message, don't think it strange if people are "put off" or "offended" by what you are trying to tell them. The Gospel is offensive to the world—the Bible shows this very clearly in scripture:

Galatians talk about the offense of the cross:

Galatians 5:11 (KJV): And I, brethren, if I yet preach circumcision, why do I yet suffer persecution? Then is the offence of the cross ceased.

In Acts, Peter and John were commanded not to speak of CHRIST:

Acts 4:18-20 (KJV): 18And they called them, and commanded them not to speak at all nor teach in the name of JESUS. 19 But Peter and John answered and said unto them, Whether it be right in the sight of GOD to hearken unto you more than unto GOD, judge ye. 20 For we cannot but speak the things which we have seen and heard.

CHRIST HIMSELF was deemed as "crazy" by his friends and family:

Mark 3:21 (NIV): When HIS family heard about this, they went to take charge of HIM, for they said, "HE is out of HIS Mind."

CHRIST's own chosen people, the Jews, turned against HIM:

Mark 15:13-14 (KJV): 13 And they cried out again, Crucify HIM. 14 Then Pilate said unto them, Why, what evil hath HE done? And they cried out the more exceedingly, Crucify HIM.

In this passage, CHRIST points out that HE suffered persecution which will not be foreign to those who follow HIM:

John 15:20 (KJV): 20 Remember the word that I said unto you, The servant is not greater than his lord. If they have persecuted ME, they will also persecute you; if they have kept MY saying, they will keep yours also.

Scripture says that CHRIST is a stumbling block to HIS OWN people and foolishness to the gentiles:

1 Corinthians 1:23 (KJV): 23But we preach CHRIST crucified, unto the Jews a stumbling block, and unto the Greeks foolishness;

This passages shows that the Cross of CHRIST is nonsense to those who are perishing apart from it:

1 Corinthians 1:18 (KJV): 18For the preaching of the Cross is to them that perish foolishness; but unto us which are saved it is the Power of GOD.

Only by the Power of the HOLY SPIRIT in someone's life will the person be moving in GOD's Will exclusively.

1 Corinthians 2:14 (KJV): 14But the natural man receiveth not the things of the SPIRIT of GOD: for they are foolishness unto him: neither can he know them, because they are SPIRITUALLY discerned.

So be aware: there is a price to pay to follow the LORD and to be HIS messenger: worth it all in the long run…

Luke 14:27 (KJV): And whosoever doth not bear his cross, and come after ME, cannot be MY disciple.

20. THE MAJORITY OF THE WORLD IS CAUGHT UP IN THEIR OWN PLEASURE: SEEKING WEALTH; SEEKING REBELLION TO GOD; SEEKING SENSUAL PLEASURES.

(Words Received from Our LORD by Susan, Novermber 19, 2013)

Children, this is your GOD. You see that the time is drawing nigh. You see I am trying to make it obvious to you but many do not want to pay attention.

Many are still enthralled by the world by what looks normal and exciting to them. The world is putrid to MY Face: it stinks and it is disgusting to ME, a Holy GOD. The world runs contrary to MY Will, the Will of GOD. The world looks right and normal, but only a few operate in MY Will.

The majority of the world is caught up in their own pleasure: seeking wealth; seeking rebellion to GOD; seeking sensual pleasures. This is not MY Will, it is the will of MY enemy. And this is who the people are led by, the enemy of GOD.

The people want to be led by MY enemy. They want to run counter to MY Will. These are the ones who will drink MY Cup of wrath when I come back for the few who really want to be in MY Will. This is MY true church, MY bride: the bride I died for and the bride I am coming for. She has clean garments and pursues ME avidly. She takes MY breath away. She is the one I am anxious for and she is the one I am coming to rescue. These are MY loyal followers, the few who really read MY Words, the few who follow ME through a relationship and those who want to be in MY Will.

This church is a remnant: there is only a small number compared to those turned against ME. I am coming to set you free, O' sacred

72

church. You must keep your eyes on ME. For anyone who wants to be part of this church, surrender your all to ME, repent of your sins, give forgiveness to all, seek MY HOLY SPIRIT in HIS Fullness, pray to be baptized in HIS SPIRIT, read MY Words daily, seek ME as your Best FRIEND. I want to hear from you all through the day. These are MY terms, MY requirements for being part of the prepared church. If you do not want to be part of MY church, prepare for MY wrath that is coming to punish this evil world. You must seek ME as your Only HOPE, because I AM mankind's ONLY HOPE.

This is the LORD GOD, YAHUSHUA HA MASHIACH

1 Corinthians 2:1 (KJV): But the natural man receiveth not the things of the SPIRIT of GOD: for they are foolishness unto him: neither can he know them, because they are spiritually discerned.

Galatians 5:16-17 (KJV): 16This I say then, Walk in the SPIRIT, and ye shall not fulfill the lust of the flesh. 17For the flesh lusteth against the SPIRIT, and the SPIRIT against the flesh: and these are contrary the one to the other: so that ye cannot do the things that ye would.

21. I CANNOT TOLERATE A WORLD THAT IS NOT INTERESTED IN HEARING ABOUT MY SACRIFICE ON THE CROSS

(Words Received from Our LORD by Susan, November 20, 2013)

Children, it is I, your GOD from heaven above. I want to give you news about MY COMING. So few are paying attention in this daunting hour—there is only a remnant paying attention. This has been foretold in MY Book that very few would be watching for ME when I come: when I come for MY bride, MY church.

Very few will be ready...very few will be watching...very few will be looking for ME with eager anticipation. Very few will have their EYES FIXED ON ME. Very few want to follow their GOD: in MY Perfect Will. Very few want to read MY Book by the Power of MY HOLY SPIRIT. Very few want a FULL OIL LAMP. Very few want to give all those around them FORGIVENESS that goes forth from their heart. Very few are REPENTANT before MY Holy Face. Very few are truly REMORSEFUL over their sin. Very few want to SEEK the HOLY SPIRIT for handling the sins of the flesh. Many want to handle their sins in their own flesh apart from the guidance of MY HOLY SPIRIT. It is only by the GUIDANCE and POWER of MY HOLY SPIRIT that anyone can conquer their flesh.

I, GOD, cannot stand how the church clings to the world. The world is an enmity to ME. I will not come back for you if you cling to both, ME and the world. The two cannot mix. The two cannot co-exist although this is the move of the world.

MY Message is an enmity to the world. I cannot tolerate a world that is not interested in hearing about MY SACRIFICE on the CROSS. I AM intolerant of those who deny MY GIFT, MY BLOOD SHED for all mankind. They can look the other way, to other paths that they think will lead to GOD, but there is only ONE path and it is by MY CROSS, MY BLOOD, MY SACRIFICE, MY DEATH, MY RESURRECTION, and MY SPIRIT in all HIS FULLNESS. Surrender to ME, lay your life down before ME, empty yourself. I want ALL of you: only by giving ME ALL of you will this transaction be made complete and then I will fill you with MY HOLY SPIRIT and you will receive the POWER from GOD on high to live out your life in MY PERFECT WILL for it. There is no other way, there are no other answers. This is what I require and those who think different will be left behind to face the worst: to face MY enemy, face the antichrist, to face MY wrath. Only you can make this choice for yourself, it is yours to make.

This is your GOD, Loving in ALL MY Ways…

Coordinating Scripture:

Luke 17:26-30 (KJV): 26 And as it was in the days of Noah, so shall it be also in the days of the SON of man. 27 They did eat, they drank, they married wives, they were given in marriage, until the day that Noah entered into the ark, and the flood came, and destroyed them all. 28 Likewise also as it was in the days of Lot; they did eat, they drank, they bought, they sold, they planted, they builded; 29 But the same day that Lot went out of Sodom it rained fire and brimstone from heaven, and destroyed them all. 30 Even thus shall it be in the day when the SON of man is revealed.

Matthew 7:22-23 (KJV): 22 Many will say to me in that day, LORD, LORD, have we not prophesied in THY name? And in THY name have cast out devils? And in THY name done many wonderful works? 23 And then will I profess unto them, I never knew you: depart from me, ye that work iniquity.

1 Corinthians 9:27 (KJV): But I keep under my body, and bring it into subjection: lest that by any means, when I have preached to others, I myself should be a castaway.

Philippians 2:12 (KJV): Wherefore, my beloved, as ye have always obeyed, not as in my presence only, but now much more in my absence, work out your own salvation with fear and trembling.

1 Peter 4:18 (KJV): And if the righteous scarcely be saved, where shall the ungodly and the sinner appear?

Matthew 7:13-14 (KJV): 13 Enter ye in at the strait gate: for wide is the gate, and broad is the way, that leadeth to destruction, and many there be which go in thereat: 14 Because strait is the gate, and narrow is the way, which leadeth unto life, and few there be that find it.

22. GOD'S JUDGEMENT OF THE LIVING

Dear Followers of CHRIST: Disregarding the FULL Character of GOD and the Abusing of GOD's Grace:

I have received letters from people that the messages I put out are too harsh: but not understanding the judgmental side of GOD and denying or ignoring it can be very dangerous. In fact, creating a "god" in your mind that is only about grace and mercy and not fear and judgment as well is creating a "god" of your own making and not understanding all facets of the True GOD. Actually the god of "only grace and mercy without judgment and fear" is a false god and those who pursue such a "god" have created an idol to worship for themselves.

GOD of the Bible is a GOD of Judgment WHO is to be feared. And something most people forget is that GOD judges the LIVING and the condition of their life...even before they are dead! Let me give you some examples:

Here are three examples of those who GOD judged: those living in the past in the Old Testament:

76

KORAH: Korah and others provoked GOD by rebelling against GOD's chosen leaders Moses and Aaron and this is what the scripture says happened: Numbers 16:28-33 (KJV): 28 And Moses said, Hereby ye shall know that the LORD hath sent me to do all these works; for I have not done them of mine own mind. 29If these men die the common death of all men, or if they be visited after the visitation of all men; then the LORD hath not sent me. 30 But if the LORD make a new thing, and the earth open her mouth, and swallow them up, with all that appertain unto them, and they go down quick into the pit; then ye shall understand that these men have provoked the LORD. 31 And it came to pass, as he had made an end of speaking all these words, that the ground clave asunder that was under them: 32 And the earth opened her mouth, and swallowed them up, and their houses, and all the men that appertained unto Korah, and all their goods. 33 They, and all that appertained to them, went down alive into the pit, and the earth closed upon them: and they perished from among the congregation.

AARON'S SONS NADAB AND ABIHU: Aaron's sons did not follow GOD's instructions and lived to regret it: Leviticus 10:1-3 (KJV): And Nadab and Abihu, the sons of Aaron, took either of them his censer, and put fire therein, and put incense thereon, and offered strange fire before the LORD, which HE commanded them not. 2 And there went out fire from the LORD, and devoured them, and they died before the LORD. 3 Then Moses said unto Aaron, This is it that the LORD spake, saying, I will be sanctified in them that come nigh me, and before all the people I will be glorified. And Aaron held his peace.

KING SAUL: King Saul did not follow GOD's commandments and King Saul did not have a good ending and even was disgraced in his burial: 1 Samuel 15:11 (KJV): It repenteth ME that I have set up Saul to be king: for he is turned back from following ME, and hath not performed MY Commandments. And it grieved Samuel; and he cried unto the Lord all night. 1 Samuel 15:26 (KJV): And Samuel said unto Saul, I will not return with thee: for thou hast rejected the Word of the Lord, and the Lord hath rejected thee from being king over Israel. 1 Samuel 15:35 (KJV): And Samuel came no more to see Saul until the day of his death: nevertheless Samuel mourned for Saul: and the Lord repented that HE had made Saul king over Israel.

Here are also three examples of those who GOD judged while living in the past New Testament:

HUSBAND AND WIFE ANANIAS AND SAPPHIRA: These Bible characters lied to the HOLY SPIRIT and did not have a chance to do anything else: Acts 5:1-5 (KJV): But a certain man named Ananias, with Sapphira his wife, sold a possession, 2 And kept back part of the price, his wife also being privy to it, and brought a certain part, and laid it at the apostles' feet. 3 But Peter said, Ananias, why hath Satan filled thine heart to lie to the HOLY GHOST, and to keep back part of the price of the land? 4 Whiles it remained, was it not thine own? and after it was sold, was it not in thine own power? Why hast thou conceived this thing in thine heart? Thou hast not lied unto men, but unto GOD. 5 And Ananias hearing these words fell down, and gave up the GHOST: and great fear came on all them that heard these things.

HEROD: Herod's fatal error was to take credit that belonged to GOD and he too was judged by GOD while he was yet alive: Acts 12:21-23 (KJV): 21 And upon a set day Herod, arrayed in royal apparel, sat upon his throne, and made an oration unto them. 22 And the people gave a shout, saying, It is the voice of a god, and not of a man. 23 And immediately the angel of the LORD smote him, because he gave not GOD the glory: and he was eaten of worms, and gave up the ghost.

Here are three more examples of those who GOD has judged while living in the future events to come foretold in the New Testament:

The False Prophet and the Antichrist: The Bible foretells the actions of the future of the living to come in Revelation 20:10 (KJV): And the devil that deceived them was cast into the lake of fire and brimstone, where the beast and the false prophet are, and shall be tormented day and night forever and ever.

And the last group already judged and sentenced to death future-tense will be the Lukewarm Church: Revelation 3:16 (KJV): So then because thou art lukewarm, and neither cold nor hot, I will spue thee out of MY Mouth.

HOW TO BE IN THE SAFETY ZONE APART FROM GOD'S JUDGEMENT OF THE LIVING:

Ephesians 4:30 (KJV): And grieve not the HOLY SPIRIT of GOD, whereby ye are sealed unto the day of redemption.

1 Thessalonians 5:19 (KJV): Quench not the SPIRIT.

Submit yourself to the Will of GOD—repent and surrender your ALL to the Will of GOD through CHRIST and ask for the Power of the HOLY SPIRIT to come into you to help you to do the Will of GOD in your life always:

Mark 3:35 (KJV): For whosoever shall do the Will of GOD, the same is MY brother, and MY sister, and mother.

John 9:31 (KJV): Now we know that GOD heareth not sinners: but if any man be a worshipper of GOD, and doeth HIS Will, him HE heareth.

Romans 12:2 (KJV): And be not conformed to this world: but be ye transformed by the renewing of your mind, that ye may prove what is that good, and acceptable, and perfect, Will of GOD.

Colossians 4:12 (KJV): Epaphras, who is one of you, a servant of CHRIST, saluteth you, always labouring fervently for you in prayers, that ye may stand perfect and complete in all the Will of GOD.

1 Peter 4:2 (KJV): That he no longer should live the rest of his time in the flesh to the lusts of men, but to the Will of GOD.

1 John 2:17 (KJV): And the world passeth away, and the lust thereof: but he that doeth the Will of GOD abideth for ever.

23. IF YOU ARE NOT IN MY WILL THEN YOU ARE NOT RIGHT WITH ME

(Words Received from Our LORD by Susan, December 3, 2013)

It is I, your GOD. I am ready to give you Words.

MY children, you must take heed. I am a GOD WHO is Truthful. The Truth must be told and I tell it. The world is spiraling down. It is rejecting its GOD. Few are really following ME the way I want to be followed. This is MY remnant, the rest remain lost far from ME. Few understand what I require to remain in MY good graces. So many believe they understand, but most men operate outside of MY Will.

It is being in MY Will that is most important. If you are not in MY Will then you are not right with ME. Only those in MY Will, will be raptured. It is those who will be saved. The others who remain outside of MY Will, will be left behind to face the worst because they have chosen to live apart from GOD.

MY Will is the ONLY safe place. There is NO OTHER safe place. If you are outside of MY Will you are being run by the enemy. And if you don't change, you are as good as dead to me. You must pursue ME at all costs. Pursue ME as if your life depends on it because it does. Pray earnestly to be in MY Will. Pray fervently to be in your GOD's Will. Your will, which is the enemy's will is a stench to ME and MY Ways. It is rebellion and treason against MY Kingdom.

Many of you will not like to hear these Words because you are unfamiliar with MY Ways. But I am a GOD of Precision and Righteousness. I do not take well to rebellion. MY rebellious children who do not change their ways will be cast away. Despite MY Love for them, I am still a Righteous JUDGE. I cannot deny WHO I am. I stand for holiness and perfection. MY Ways are Perfect and MY Love is always Perfect.

If you think this is a hard Word. Who can walk on this path? Only those who surrender to MY Will. Those who surrender to MY Will: they become perfect through the Power of MY HOLY SPIRIT, and by the Blood that I gave on Calvary. MY Blood covers your imperfection, MY SPIRIT guides you to all Truth, and I lead you out to safety. There is NO other path.

Today you must make a choice. If you want to be near ME and MY Safety, you must decide to be in MY Will. I want you to choose for ME. I want you to choose to give ME your all. I want you to lay your life down before ME, repent of your former ways and sin. Come with a remorseful heart for living apart from MY Will. I want you to see living for the world and MY enemy is not the correct path to MY Will. It is a broad road to hell to which many, even most are going.

Very few want to be in their GOD's Will. Only a remnant really pursue MY Will. Let me show you the Way: surrender your all to ME and I will give you ALL of ME. Come into MY Saving Grace, and Power, and live the life you were meant to live. Be prepared and make ready for MY Coming, as this hour is closing in and as the world is descending into complete darkness apart from its love and respect for ME and MY Ways. I change not. I am the Unchanging GOD. Pursue ME and be saved.

This is the GOD of Your Salvation

I am the NARROW PATH

Coordinating Scripture:

Matthew 7:21-23 (KJV): 21 Not everyone that saith unto ME, LORD, LORD, shall enter into the kingdom of heaven; but he that doeth the Will of MY FATHER which is in heaven. 22 Many will say to ME in that day, LORD, LORD, have we not prophesied in THY Name? And in THY Name have cast out devils? And in THY Name done many wonderful works? 23 And then will I profess unto them, I never knew you: depart from me, ye that work iniquity.

1 Samuel 15:23 (KJV): For rebellion is as the sin of witchcraft, and stubbornness is as iniquity and idolatry. Because thou hast rejected the Word of the LORD, HE hath also rejected thee from being king.

Romans 12:2 (KJV): And be not conformed to this world: but be ye transformed by the renewing of your mind, that ye may prove what is that good, and acceptable, and perfect, Will of GOD.

Matthew 7:14 (KJV): Because strait is the gate, and narrow is the way, which leadeth unto life, and few there be that find it.

(Doing good is not always "good" as seen in Matthew 7:21-23. The people prophesied, worked wonders, and cast out demons and yet they were still considered workers of iniquity because they were found outside of the Will of GOD. Here is more about the Knowledge of Good:

http://lovethewhirlwind.wordpress.com/2010/02/21/knowledge-of-good/

24. YOU MUST COME TO ME NOW !

Donna McDonald received Prophetic Words for Watchman Radio Listeners in the UK Hosted by Minister Curtis Roach for 12/3/13:

I (Donna) have gotten on the floor and knelt with my head covered and pleaded with the LORD for the listeners and asked HIM, Dear LORD, do you have Words for the listeners of the Watchman Radio Program? This is HIS reply (Here is the radio show link: http://youtu.be/T72vrhpkkJ8 http://youtu.be/T72vrhpkkJ8 :

Yes, Daughter I have Words for you to deliver to the listeners. This is your LORD speaking, YAHUSHUA HA MASHIACH, Amen.

Dear Children, I Am the LORD GOD ALMIGHTY, the MAKER of the heaven and earth.

I come to you through the voice of MY servant, Donna. She is to deliver this message to you. She is meek and of ME and this is why I chose her to deliver this message. She pursues ME and MY FATHER and the HOLY SPIRIT with all of her heart. Children, this is the LORD speaking. You must come to ME NOW. I am pleading with you in these last hours. These are the last hours before I make MY mark on this earth. I am going to let the floodgates open and let the enemy have his way with this earth soon. The earth will be given over to him and it is just a matter of a short time. There is not much time left and you must be on the alert. You are MY enemy if you do not listen to this message and fold into ME and MY plan for you. You must listen very closely for I am your GOD and I have your best interests in mind. I am not here to tickle your ears or to placate you or pat you on your back. There are many of MY children perishing every day while you are looking on your ipods, your computers, and your screens of all sorts. YOU are MY warriors, MY end time warriors and I Am CALLING YOU to battle. You must put down your weapons of the world that will go soft in battle and pick up MY Weapons. MY Weapons are ones that the world does not identify with. These are MY Weapons:

1. Humility—you must be a humble warrior—put on the cloak of humility. I cannot have a warrior that is prideful and wants their own way. MY warriors must listen to MY Call and MY Orders to be right with ME and to lead the sheep into the correct pasture.

2. Love—you must, must, must love your neighbor. This is literal. You must go out of your way to show love and kindness to those around you. This is a method that throws the enemy off of your path. He cannot track you and keep up with you when you show LOVE. It is with LOVE that I allowed MYSELF to be crucified and it is with LOVE that MY FATHER sent ME to earth to suffer for you once and for all.

3. Generosity—you must be generous with your time and resources. If someone admires something you have or something you use or own just give it to them. Tell them you will not need it anyway because your LORD will be coming back soon for the rapture and you are betting your money and your valuables on that.

4. Earnestness—be true and earnest to your word. If you say something let it be the Truth.

5. Fidelity—let your life speak for and of ME. If you are true to your word and you walk closely with ME and you walk for ME then you will show the world you are a person of your word and your word means you are of ME. People will listen when you walk with fidelity.

6. Commitment—be committed to your GOD. Everything you do must be a reflection of your relationship with ME. If you are of ME and in ME then what you do will reflect ME.

7. SPIRIT—you must be filled with MY HOLY SPIRIT in order to have the dunamis you need, the power you need to complete the tasks I have given you, your assignment from ME in this fallen world.

It is simple to be filled with the HOLY SPIRIT. The enemy wants MY Filling to sound like an enigma and make it mysterious, but it is not, it is simple. Just pray earnestly that you would like to be filled with MY HOLY SPIRIT and I will come into you and fill you up. As you submit your will to ME, as I educate you on MY Ways, then you will stay filled. It is not enough to invite ME to fill you, you must continue to search ME out and submit to ME and I will continue to keep you filled. It is like a hot air balloon that needs the heat to stay full and light, and in the air, so the same with the HOLY SPIRIT. You need

MY Heat, MY Fire, MY HOLY SPIRIT to stay full and fulfilled to do MY Work.

8. Daily Walk—You must pursue ME daily, your GOD, to be in MY Will. You must stay in MY Will in order to do MY Work. Pursue ME by reading MY Word as early as possible in the day, read and then pray to ME. Call out to ME for your loved ones, and the ones you have shared and witnessed to and I will hear your prayers, your cries, and intervene for you to MY FATHER in heaven WHO waits to hear MY every breath and MY every Word to call out to HIM for MY children and intervene for you on behalf of your prayer requests.

England and Great Britain and the rest of the world. These words are for you. These are MY Words. I want you to take them to heart. I have recited them to MY servant, Donna, for your benefit and edification. I intend for each of you to take these to heart. They line up with scripture so do not quibble over a phrase or preposition and say this does not sound like the GOD you know. Look at the body of a prophesy—is the message clear and succinct and does it line up with the scriptures that you know from MY Book and MY Words?

I am your GOD, your Loving FATHER, your Hope in this dark, dark, world. The world is spiraling down and I Am giving MY Words and Ways out to MY prophets. You must listen and take heed lest you be left behind and everyone who is dear to you will suffer as well and be taken captive by MY enemy. THIS IS THE GREATEST BATTLE OF YOUR LIFE. THERE WILL BE NO BIGGER BATTLE THAN THE ONE FOR YOUR VERY SOUL. If you have served in the military in WW2 such as the Battle of the Bulge or the Battle in Afghanistan or in Iran or Iraq or Korea or Vietnam or any other war you will not know warfare like you will know when you are enlightened of the stealthiness of the enemy, satan. He knows no boundaries and no limits and he knows no international treaties or limits of war. He does not fight with a conscience or within international laws. He fights dirty. He fights with no remorse. He fights like he is there to win at all costs. He is a stealthy victor in many battles. There is ONE THING he needs to know, though. MY army, MY warriors are one step ahead of him. They have the Power of the HOLY SPIRIT and of love, and the Word, and of humility, and peace. MY Army fights with weapons that satan is not skilled at using and will behave as if he has never heard of them or seen them. MY enemy will be rendered useless when you fight, take up the battle with the Weapons I have identified in this Body of Work.

You do not have to be young and physically strong to be MY Warriors. Some of MY generals, seven starred, are the most feeble little ladies you have ever seen. They are in nursing homes and rest homes and they spend their days offering up condolences for humanity and call out to ME, their GOD, for the salvation of those around them. You want to know who will be around ME in heaven? Well it won't be the likes of the Internet or TV preachers who talk about money, money, money, or have their names plastered all over everything they publish. The people who will be around ME in heaven will be the little people that no one paid attention to and the people thought to be crazy because they pursued me like a comet on fire. They were all over ME on earth and pursued ME like I was the ONLY Answer in their life to their problems and their longings to be near ME in heaven.

Do not persecute this daughter, this prophet of MINE. If you do not like this message then you get with ME and pray to ME for the answers to your questions. I Am a GOD that desires each of you, MY children, to hear MY Voice but first I want to hear yours. I want you to go hoarse in your spirit calling out to ME in prayer and supplication for yourself and those around you. You have plenty of time to pray—every stoplight, every train stop, every bus ride, every walk, every bike ride, every moment you push a stroller. When you stand at the kitchen sink, the bathroom sink, in the shower like MY son Buddy Baker whom I give great visions in the shower. I don't care if you are unclothed, clothed, or smelly and dirty. I made you and I created you and I want you just as you are. This is one thing, my son Billy Graham got right is you are to come, "just as I am" to ME. One other thing you and he need to get right is that you must have a complete and total filling of MY HOLY SPIRIT in order to be right with ME. A half-filled oil lamp or half-portion of MY HOLY SPIRIT will not do. It will not make you lighter than air and it will not lift you to the heavenlies when I come for MY Rapture of MY bride, the church. MY bride is beautiful and she is white and radiant and perfect for Me because she has prepared herself and made herself beautiful to ME in all her ways. Let ME count them, the ways…How does she love ME?

1. She is a radiant bride—she has made herself holy and beautiful. She shuns all worldly things because she knows they are distasteful to her GROOM.

2. She pursues ME with all of her heart and being. This is how she shows ME she loves ME. She is thinking of ME 24/7 as I Am her First LOVE and Only LOVE. O' you may love your spouse, or fiancé, or your children, or parents, or siblings, but you must love ME more and desire ME more. As you commit yourself to ME this longing for ME will grow stronger.

3. She reads MY Love Letters to her. These letters are called the Old Testament and New Testament. You understand this, it is self-explanatory.

4. She worships and praises MY Name. This does not have to be done by a tenor or soprano or public speaker. She can praise me

with her simple small voice that is off key or hoarse or tired or not feeling well. She can praise ME with a few words or many words for I know her heart. When she is tired or ill I know a few words will suffice for I know her heart. A smile from the heart goes a long way with your GOD.

5. She shows ME she loves ME by going out of her way for others. She can do this with a baby in arms or a toddler or sick parent or at work. She does not have to schedule it though she may put this activity of loving others on her calendar. I Am not all about works but I am about MY FATHER's Business which is bringing others to ME and then to Him. Only those who come to ME will ever share the presence of MY FATHER, MY O' so Holy FATHER in heaven. Going out of your way for others does not have to be long and tedious. O', no. Just pick something up from the ground for them, pay a few extra cents in line that someone needs, turn around to someone standing beside you or sitting next to you. Speak loving or positive words to those. Then you may say that GOD loves you very much and I want you to know that we are in the end times and He is coming back soon for HIS church, HIS bride, and HE wants you to go with HIM and not be left behind. This is how you can assure yourself you will not be left behind. Give them the "Marriage Supper of the Lamb" link. You can print it on a business card and pass it out or you can verbally speak it to them to copy or write it on a scratch piece of note book paper. You can record it anywhere or any way you like. It is the most succinct body of Truth in how to be prepared for MY soon coming that is in print. I have personally ordained this body of work by the power of MY HOLY SPIRIT to Susan Davis when she was on a forty-day fast. MY daughter, Donna, works with Susan. They are ministry partners under ME and the HOLY SPIRIT. One is the mouth, one is the set of hands, but they both make up a body that works for MY purposes in these end times.

This daughter has faithfully recorded these Words for you, the listeners of Minister Curtis Roach's radio hour in the UK but these Words are for all believers and all those who want to be rapture ready for your soon coming KING.

This is the LORD speaking, YAHUSHUA HA MASHIACH. Amen, Amen, Amen. Let those wedding bells Ring, Ring, Ring. Amen.

Signed, Sealed, and Delivered with a Holy Kiss from your CREATOR. Amen.

25. IF YOU ARE CAUGHT UP IN THE WAYS OF THE WORLD YOU WILL BE LEFT

(Words Received from Our LORD by Susan, December 13, 2013)

Children, it is I, your GOD, I am here to give you more Words:

There is a definite change in the atmosphere. Look around you, it is everywhere. The people are oblivious to MY Coming, but MY SPIRIT-filled ones see it: those who know their GOD; those who spend time with ME in the secret place; those who read their Bibles daily; those who share MY SPIRIT. They see with MY Eyes what is going on in the world.

I am coming to pull out those who are watching, ONLY those who watch. All others who are handling the world will be left. If you are caught up in the ways of the world you will be left. This is a hard Word but it is MY Truth. Read MY Book and see for yourself. If you knew ME, you would know this is Truth. Only those who are standing close to ME will be seen by ME and be taken when I come back for MY own.

These are the ones I desire to be with for eternity, the ones I will call MY bride, the ones I will share nuptials with. These are the ones who will be with ME as MY bride for eternity. Those who are left behind can come to ME later, but they will not be MY bride and many will fall away in sudden destruction without any hope of recovery.

This is a SERIOUS WORD, MY children. You must know that I am a GOD of TRUTH. You must also know that I am a GOD WHO cannot be played with. Do not try ME or MY Patience. Yes, I am long suffering but don't reject the price that was paid for you on the Cross for long or you may miss your chance for salvation.

These are serious Words for serious times. MY Coming is soon. Sober up, get ready, prepare your garments, focus on ME. I am your ONLY HOPE. Surrender your all to ME, surrender to MY Will. Repent to your GOD for past evil, read MY Book everyday, pray for your neighbors and loved ones and pray that you may be found worthy at MY Coming. These Words are Truth, I am a GOD of Truth.

This is the LORD on High

Coordinating Scripture:

Psalm 91 (KJV): He that dwelleth in the secret place of the Most HIGH shall abide under the Shadow of the ALMIGHTY.

Revelation 16:15 (KJV): Behold, I come as a thief. Blessed is he that watcheth, and keepeth his garments, lest he walk naked, and they see his shame.

James 4:4 (KJV): Ye adulterers and adulteresses, know ye not that the friendship of the world is enmity with GOD? Whosoever therefore will be a friend of the world is the enemy of GOD.

Matthew 22:1-14:—The Parable of the King's Wedding for His Son

26. NO ONE WILL BE SAFE FROM THE DOMINATION OF EVIL MAN RUN BY EVIL SPIRITS

(Words Received from Our LORD by Susan, December 15, 2013)

Dear Children, This is your LORD. I AM coming and NO one can stop ME. Some believe I will not ever come. Some believe I am not coming for a long time. Some think of ME as a far off GOD. I am none of these. I am coming with MY mighty angel army. I am going to split the skies open with the beauty of MY Majesty and MY Presence. Those watching will see ME first. They will see their KING make a grand entrance.

The stage will be set for the removal of MY bride to lift her up into the skies out of harm's way. She will follow ME out to safety. I will pull her free. There will be mass hysteria. People will run everywhere wondering what has happened because of the devastation and missing people. There will be many explanations for what has taken place. Most will be inspired by evil, who want to down play MY Coming.

The world will not be the same. It will be the start of a new era—the onset of the antichrist kingdom in full force: man's way of coping with the aftermath of the removal of MY bride from the earth. Once MY bride is taken free and MY SPIRIT is taken out of the way, the enemy's kingdom will come into power in full force and no one will be safe from the domination of evil man run by evil spirits from the kingdom of darkness.

Horror will reign on earth as I allow MY wrath to pour over the earth. Tribulation will reign supreme—Great Tribulation. MY children who are left behind will face their darkest hour. Dark decisions will be theirs to make choosing between the antichrist system which leads ultimately to eternal doom or choosing against the commanding system leading to their martyrdom. Many will be tortured and suffer greatly in order to escape the kingdom of darkness that will rule the earth and all who remain behind.

You can avoid this end—turn to ME now as your only hope. Give ME your all in all—full surrender of your will into MY Hands. I will protect you, guide you, keep you in MY Will if you so desire to be MINE. Just surrender, repent, and submit yourself over to ME. All will be well between us. I will protect you from the coming evil: a system that is even now in the works.

Please turn your life over to ME. I am pleading with you children. Walk with your GOD into safekeeping.

I AM GOD...I AM ALL KNOWING...ALL SEEING...ALPHA & OMEGA...

BEGINNING and the END

Coordinating Scripture:

Acts 1:11 (KJV): Which also said, Ye men of Galilee, why stand ye gazing up into heaven? This same JESUS, which is taken up from you into heaven, shall so come in like manner as ye have seen HIM go into heaven.

Luke 17:24 (KJV): For as the lightning, that lighteneth out of the one part under heaven, shineth unto the other part under heaven; so shall also the SON of man be in HIS day.

Luke 21:36 (KJV): Watch ye therefore, and pray always, that ye may be accounted worthy to escape all these things that shall come to pass, and to stand before the SON of man.

2 Thessalonians 2:7 (KJV): For the mystery of iniquity doth already work: only HE WHO now letteth will let, until HE be taken out of the way.

Revelation 14:9-10 (KJV): 9 And the third angel followed them, saying with a loud voice, If any man worship the beast and his image, and receive his mark in his forehead, or in his hand, 10 The same shall drink of the wine of the wrath of GOD, which is poured out without mixture into the cup of his indignation; and he shall be tormented with fire and brimstone in the presence of the holy angels, and in the presence of the LAMB:

27. I WILL MULTIPLY MY SIGNS AND WONDERS

The LORD's Words for Today

Locusts; frogs; dead cattle; water turned into blood; lice; hail; boils; and overwhelming darkness did not shake lose the heart of the Pharaoh to release the Israelites. Exodus 7:3 (KJV) reads: And I will harden Pharaoh's heart, and multiply MY signs and MY wonders in the land of Egypt....Exodus 7:14 (KJV) says: And the LORD said unto Moses, Pharaoh's heart is hardened, he refuseth to let the people go. And Exodus 8:15 (KJV) says: But when Pharaoh saw that there was respite, he hardened his heart, and hearkened not unto them; as the LORD had said.

Who doesn't marvel at Pharaoh's hard-hearted stubbornness to endure such calamity and still block the release of the Israelites from leaving Egypt? You've got to think this guy had to be really living on the river "denial."

Over and over the Egyptians witnessed the worst disasters and calamity and yet their leader would not budge to heed the warnings of GOD! WOW—what does this remind you of? Does it sound like the absolute image of how the lukewarm church and the secular world refuses to believe the multiple "signs" and warnings in the Bible for this generation that won't pass away until all these things are fulfilled prior to the rapture of the bride of CHRIST?

How is it that the Bible signs written 2,000 years ago can come together, and yet the people reject GOD and HIS warnings to surrender and to be ready for CHRIST's Return?

According to the Bible, the enemy of mankind, satan is playing a role In the blinding of men's eyes. 2 Corinthians 4:3-4 (KJV): But if our gospel be hid, it is hid to them that are lost: In whom the god of this world hath blinded the minds of them which believe not, lest the light of the glorious gospel of CHRIST, WHO is the IMAGE of GOD, should shine unto them.

And it also says in the Bible that all the knowledge men seek apart from GOD will corrupt and blind them to the Truth: 2 Timothy 3:7-8 (KJV): Ever learning, and never able to come to the knowledge of the truth. 8 Now as Jannes and Jambres withstood Moses, so do these also resist the truth: men of corrupt minds, reprobate concerning the faith.

The Bible also says that GOD (like HE did with Pharaoh) will put it in the hearts of men to do HIS Will: Revelation 17:17 (KJV): For GOD hath put in their hearts to fulfil HIS Will, and to agree, and give their kingdom unto the beast, until the Words of GOD shall be fulfilled.

Here are more websites with the UNDENIABLE evidence the LORD's predicted coming is just moments away:

http://bibleprobe.com/end-time-signs.htm

http://www.signs-of-end-times.com/

28. HOW SHALL I CALL YOU? MY BRIDE OR MY LEFT BEHIND LOST CHURCH?

(Words Received from Our LORD by Susan, December 31, 2013)

My Children this is your GOD:

I want to address you about the near future: The world continues to increase in darkness. The hearts of the people grow shallow—they are walking in lust; cold from lack of love; pierced by the arrows of the enemy who wants to destroy them. Men's hearts are waxing cold. I said this would happen and now the Truth has come to pass. The people have forgotten how to blush. They are so cold they have no compassion for their neighbors.

My church is the light in a dark world—she follows her GOD closely—she sees the truth while the lost run from the truth and scurries to the darkness out of sight. My church is bold in her testimony of ME. The lost deny I exist and look for reasons to explain ME away. MY church understands true love and what commitment and longsuffering looks like. MY church is persecuted in this evil world and the world is an enmity to MY church. She has MY heart and looks like ME. She is not attracted by the ways and desires of a dying world. The world is unclean and abominable to her. She has no interest in absorbing into the ways of a world that has turned its back to GOD. She resists the temptation to conform to a world that follows the on heals of MY enemy. Her eyes have been washed out with eye salve and she has been purified by MY blood, walks in Truth, and exhibits the traits of her GOD: Love; compassion; caring; longsuffering; peace; and joy. Only MY SPIRIT's Power enables her to look like ME in front of a dying world. She has MY SPIRIT in full and her lamp shines brightly. She walks on paths of Light and shines with MY Truth in a deep dark world. She stands out among the wolves in sheep's clothing, the lost, the goats.

This is MY bride—prepared and ready for MY Coming because she is watching and her face is turned toward her GOD. This is what separates her from the world: a heart of pure gold. Carry on MY faithful bride—the world, the skies, these things speak of MY coming even when the hearts of men deny MY Coming is true. Soon the lost left behind will repent with sadness over the plight they are facing apart from the HOLY SPIRIT removed from the world allowing the man of perdition to step forward and to terrorize mankind. Be ready children—how shall I call you? MY bride or MY left behind lost church? You decide—who do you want to spend eternity with? ME or MY enemy—there is only one choice and this is yours to make. Time is short. Always be prepared for MY coming.

The is the LORD YAHUSHUA

BRILLIANT LIGHT—The BRIGHT and MORNING STAR

Coordinating Scripture:

Matthew 25:32-33 (KJV): And before HIM shall be gathered all nations: and HE shall separate them one from another, as a shepherd divideth his sheep from the goats: 33 And HE shall set the sheep on HIS right Hand, but the goats on the left.

2 Thessalonians 2:7-8 (KJV): For the mystery of iniquity doth already work: only HE WHO now letteth will let, until HE be taken out of the way.8 And then shall that wicked be revealed, whom the LORD shall consume with the SPIRIT of HIS Mouth, and shall destroy with the Brightness of HIS Coming:

2 Thessalonians 2:3 (KJV): 3 Let no man deceive you by any means: for that day shall not come, except there come a falling away first, and that man of sin be revealed, the son of perdition;

29. THOSE WHO FIGHT AGAINST ME AND MY WORDS WILL FIND THEY CANNOT WIN

(Words Received from Our LORD by Susan, January 6, 2014)

Let US begin:

Children, it is I, your LORD speaking: There are frightening things coming around the bend. Man has refused to grasp what is coming so near. Although I have outlined for them in the Words I have written so long ago, the people still want to believe differently. MY Words are true—they are perfect—they are on time—they are ready to come about. Many of these words have already come about—you are witnessing them daily—yet so many sleep, so many slumber. Sleeping: this is how I find MY dead church, MY lukewarm dead— those who refuse to believe they are living in the last days before the calamity that is about to befall the earth.

Children, you are playing with fire when you refuse to listen to MY warnings and MY messengers. These events are set in time to awaken you, to stir you to action. Yes it is causing many to awaken and stir but not enough. Soon people will be wanting to pursue their

GOD as they see more and more pointing to my "soon return." I do not want to leave anyone behind, but MY Words are clear and I must be true to MY Word. If you are not submitted to ME, surrendered heart, soul, mind, and spirit with a truly repentant heart, then you are not carrying a full oil lamp and you will be overlooked when I come back for MY own.

Most are not paying attention and most do not want what I have to offer. The people would much rather play with the things of the world then to come looking for their GOD. Soon they will see that the latter choice is the safe place and the scoffers and naysayers will be silenced by the Truth and reality of the events that are about to unfold. Yet, I continue to cry out to MY lost sheep and MY Heart wrenches over the many who will be lost: both to a dark world led by MY enemy to the slaughter and to the even darker world—eternal hell. I do not want a single soul lost but MY Truth and MY Word are constant and those who fight against ME and MY Words will find they cannot win.

Come to the LIGHT, MY Truth, and MY soon rescue—don't let the darkness come between us. Come let me expose your dark parts to the light and clean you up, make you ready. This is MY Greatest Desire to have a pure and ready bride so that I can take her home with ME to MY heavenlies. Are you ready? Will you come away with ME when I call for you—will you even hear MY Voice? Are you watching for ME, longing for ME and MY soon return? This is something you need to decide. Don't put off what needs to be done now and not later—your attention to your own salvation and the condition of your soul and the outcome of your future for all eternity. Will you spend it with your GOD, your CREATOR? Or will you be lost in the eternal abyss with the enemy—the great deceiver? You must choose and no choice is a choice against me. I pray you will make your way to ME, now—as you need ME more than you know.

Come quickly, come under MY saving mantle and blood covering. It is yours, just for the asking. Let these Words permeate your soul into action.

I am the LORD YEHUSHUA—MAKER of All

Coordinating Scripture:

2 Timothy 3:16 (KJV): All scripture is given by inspiration of GOD, and is profitable for doctrine, for reproof, for correction, for instruction in righteousness:

Matthew 25:5 (KJV): While the BRIDEGROOM tarried, they all slumbered and slept.

Revelation 3:19 (KJV): As many as I love, I rebuke and chasten: be zealous therefore, and repent.

Deuteronomy 6:5 (KJV): And thou shalt love the LORD thy GOD with all thine heart, and with all thy soul, and with all thy might.

Romans 10:3 (KJV): For they being ignorant of GOD's righteousness, and going about to establish their own righteousness, have not submitted themselves unto the righteousness of GOD.

30. SO JUST WHAT IS THE STATE OF YOUR SPIRITUAL CONDITION?

Dear Followers of CHRIST:

One of the saddest moments for mankind is the part in the Bible where it says in Genesis 3:24: So HE drove out the man... GOD had to send Adam and Eve away from HIS presence—a very sad time for human kind. Man departed from the Divine and had to settle for moving away toward outer darkness away from the GIVER of life.

Genesis 3:22-24 (KJV): 22 And the LORD GOD said, Behold, the man is become as one of US, to know good and evil: and now, lest he put forth his hand, and take also of the tree of life, and eat, and live forever: 23 Therefore the LORD GOD sent him forth from the garden of Eden, to till the ground from whence he was taken. 24 So HE drove out the man; and HE placed at the east of the garden of Eden Cherubims, and a flaming sword which turned every way, to keep the way of the tree of life.

Then in Genesis 4:16, we see again after reading that Cain has killed his brother Abel, the Bible says: "And Cain went out from the presence of the LORD."

Genesis 4:16 (KJV): And Cain went out from the presence of the LORD, and dwelt in the land of Nod, on the east of Eden.

How much sadder could this be that men had to leave the presence of GOD and we have been away from HIM ever since caught up in a world filled with sin and under a curse. Very few find their way back to GOD wholeheartedly and most pursue the things of the world.

102

Some have made it back to GOD—Abraham believed GOD, the Bible says and GOD counted it as righteousness for his belief in GOD.

Romans 4:3 (KJV): For what saith the scripture? Abraham believed GOD, and it was counted unto him for righteousness.

Noah, it says in Genesis 6:8, found grace in the eyes of the LORD.

Genesis 6:8 (KJV): But Noah found grace in the eyes of the LORD.

The Bible says that as soon as Daniel set his heart toward GOD to understand HIM then GOD listened to the words of Daniel for GOD.

Daniel 10:12 (KJV): Then said he unto me, Fear not, Daniel: for from the first day that thou didst set thine heart to understand, and to chasten thyself before thy GOD, thy words were heard, and I am come for thy words.

So just what is the state of your spiritual condition? Are you like Cain moving away from GOD's presence into the land of Nod OR are you trying to be like Abraham, Noah, and Daniel pursuing GOD and HIS Heart? When you move away from CHRIST toward pursuit of the world you are moving away from the Life GIVER, the ONE WHO created it all. Ultimately—most of mankind separates itself from GOD eternally when they choose against HIM. If you aren't striving daily to seek after GOD because you are more interested in the world and what you think it offers, you may find yourself in a condition that you can't recover from by grieving the HOLY SPIRIT. Don't leave anything to chance when it comes to where you spend eternity...

31. GET TO KNOW ME AS YOUR ONLY HOPE, AS THERE IS NO OTHER HOPE FOR THIS LOST WORLD BUT ME, ITS GOD, ITS MAKER.

(Words Received from Our LORD by Susan, January 12, 2014)

I am ready to begin a new letter:

Children, this is your GOD—I am coming soon to wipe the tears away from those who love ME, who are watching for ME, who are loyal to ME. Soon all the woes of this world will leave you far behind. I will pull you free and place you on MY firm foundation within MY Kingdom. All the sadness and losses that have come from carrying your cross for ME will be behind you as you make your way into the next life.

You are just a stranger in a foreign land—you are just passing through. This world is not your home—it is not your permanent residence. Many do not see how temporal this life is—it is a breeze, a breath, and then it is over. This is why it is dangerous to leave so much to chance and to disregard the condition of your spirit and preparations for the next life—your eternal outcome. Many just leave these decisions to be addressed at a future time and so many are taken by surprise when their lives end suddenly and their time on earth was shorter than they imagined. This is a dangerous scenario, MY children—one that the enemy is banking on that you will be foolish like the five foolish virgins caught without a full oil lamp and found unready when the bridegroom came. Don't be like these foolish virgins letting life take over from making preparations for your eternal destination. Are you coming out with ME when I return for MY loyal church—MY bride? Or are you settling for the ending that comes to those left behind or worse: caught in sudden destruction or worldly disaster? You need to take inventory of your

104

life—who do you belong to? Who do you want to belong to? Where do you want to spend eternity? You will spend it somewhere—either with ME in eternal bliss or apart from ME in agony with MY enemy. This is not a joke as so many before you have already learned. Their less than enthusiastic interest in their GOD led them down paths of darkness—darkness that never ends.

Get to know your GOD. Come find out WHO I AM, what I AM all about. Learn what I require to be ready for the next life; what you must do to be MY disciple and to lead a holy life for ME in this life surrendered to MY Perfect Will for your life. Soon, there will be a multitude of people stunned at the change of a world gone mad under the harsh leadership of evil men directed by evil spirits. Don't wait to be left behind, face ME your GOD, now. Get to know ME as your ONLY HOPE, as there is no other hope for this lost world but ME, its GOD, its MAKER. Come quickly, the hour of your salvation awaits you. Learn Bible truths through MY Word and meet with ME in the secret place to know your GOD better. These are all requirements of being ready. This is your CREATOR, the LOVER of your soul. MY Love can only be experienced when you choose to pursue it with all your heart...

Coordinating Scripture:

Revelation 21:4 (KJV): And GOD shall wipe away all tears from their eyes; and there shall be no more death, neither sorrow, nor crying, neither shall there be any more pain: for the former things are passed away.

Ephesians 2:19 (KJV): Now therefore ye are no more strangers and foreigners, but fellow citizens with the saints, and of the household of GOD;

James 4:14 (KJV): Whereas ye know not what shall be on the morrow. For what is your life? It is even a vapour, that appeareth for a little time, and then vanisheth away.

Matthew 25:3 (KJV): They that were foolish took their lamps, and took no oil with them:

1 Thessalonians 5:3 (KJV): For when they shall say, Peace and safety; then sudden destruction cometh upon them, as travail upon a woman with child; and they shall not escape.

Matthew 7:13 (KJV): Enter ye in at the strait gate: for wide is the gate, and broad is the way, that leadeth to destruction, and many there be which go in thereat:

Deuteronomy 11:13 (KJV): And it shall come to pass, if ye shall hearken diligently unto MY commandments which I command you this day, to love the LORD your GOD, and to serve HIM with all your heart and with all your soul,

32. THERE IS GREAT DARKNESS COMING OVER THE EARTH, DARKNESS BROUGHT ON BY WHOLE-HEARTED REJECTION OF GOD

(Words Received from Our LORD by Susan, January 17, 2014)

Children, it is I, your GOD.

I am standing before you with MY Arms open wide. I have nothing but love for you who keep to MY Commandments and follow MY Precepts. I am a GOD of rules and order. Very few want to accept this and disregard the rules of MY Book and the clear pathway laid out before them. Sin is sin. The sin of this world has reached an "all-time" high. It is so thick and so deep that mankind has moved into a new era of depravity.

When will it all stop? Not before I return on MY white steed to vanquish evil with the sword of MY Mouth. The world is a stench to MY Holiness. It does not want MY Truth and all that I stand for. It wants that which MY enemy sets out for it to consume. The world has engaged in the worst kind of evil and it is not slowing down.

I represent purity and all that comes from a pure, faithful heart. I am faithful to those who pursue ME. I do not go back on MY Promises: for those who draw near ME, I will draw near them. When I, GOD make a promise, I, GOD keep it. This world is full of promise-breakers. Soon those who trample MY Good Words and Good Name will know what they have done. All will be laid out when it comes time to stand before ME.

I am ready to bring out MY bride from these evil doers and those who trample MY ways. This evil people and those who cast lots with evil will remain behind to suffer the price of rebellion to a Holy GOD. There is great darkness coming over the earth, darkness brought on by whole-hearted rejection of GOD, WHO represents Truth and the Kingdom of Righteousness.

Stand firm MY children: those who pursue MY Will and follow close behind ME. You will not be disappointed in your choosing of ME and MY Ways. Your path will be made straight and your way made clear. There is much waiting for you in MY heavenlies: beauty, pleasure, love, and an environment of purity. This is MY gift for MY devoted followers: MY bride who loves ME despite her persecution and the heavy cross burden she bears for ME. All will be worth it in the long run which is sooner than you think.

Please put your focus on ME now. Stop choosing against ME for this dark world. There will be no rewards for those in the next life who love evil in this life—only eternal loss, torment, disgrace, torture, and endless darkness. This is the plight of those who reject their GOD. Come out from among them. Turn back to your GOD—find peace, wholeness, and happiness right in the midst of an evil world. It can be yours if you lay your life down at MY feet, repent of your sin and evil, turn your will and future plans over to MY Perfect Will and Plans for your life. Walk with ME and I will lead you to streams of living water. This is MY Promise. I am coming sooner than you think. Be on guard.

This is your LORD and SAVIOR—I am the LILY OF THE VALLEY—THE BRIGHT AND SHINING STAR

Coordinating Scripture:

John 14:21 (KJV): He that hath MY commandments, and keepeth them, he it is that loveth ME: and he that loveth ME shall be loved of MY FATHER, and I will love him, and will manifest MYSELF to him.

Revelation 19:11 (KJV): And I saw heaven opened, and behold a white horse; and HE that sat upon him was called FAITHFUL and TRUE, and in righteousness HE doth judge and make war.

Revelation 19:15 (KJV): And out of HIS Mouth goeth a sharp sword, that with it HE should smite the nations: and HE shall rule them with a rod of iron: and HE treadeth the winepress of the fierceness and wrath of Almighty GOD.

33. I AM THE ONE AND ONLY CURE FOR A WORLD THAT IS DYING IN ITS SIN

(Words Received from Our LORD by Susan, January 29, 2014)

I will give you new Words:

Children, it is I, your LORD. Soon you will know that I, GOD am the ONE and ONLY True GOD—there is only MYSELF and any other god is a god of manmade origin. People are looking for answers. They are looking under every rock under the sun for answers to their hardest questions. Only I offer the Truth—only I can answer all of life's hard questions. I am the RULER of the Universe. I hold the key to every question—every unknown can be known through ME, GOD.

Look, and search all you want, but I am the ONE and ONLY CURE for a world that is dying in its sin. MY BEING, MY PRESENCE is essential to life. Without MY Intervention in the world—all would die out, as I sustain ALL life. Yet, MY creation fails to acknowledge ME—the vast majority wants to disregard ME, MY Truth, MY Commands and Rules for living. Without these, mankind has no baseline for living—no standard, no guidelines. Even the world's standards are not pure and without purity the world becomes a harsh and cold place.

Children, the hour has come for you to wash your robes….they are filthy and need to be scrubbed. Don't be fooled by what your church and others say. Your robes need serious cleaning to pull you free when I come to retrieve MY bride. She can show you the ways to seek GOD. She is MY loyal church—humbly following her GOD—disassociating herself from the world. She is MY light in a dark place and MY hope for mankind rests on her willingness to follow ME.

Stay strong O' church, MY bride. I will continue to keep your lamps full—rest easy on MY Shoulders. I am fully able to deliver you from this harsh world. In closing, I want to remind you what I require to be MY bride: humility, childlike faith, humble spirit, Truth-telling. These are traits of MY few who are coming with ME when I pull you free.

This is your GOD—LORD and SAVIOR—CHRIST, The MESSIAH

Coordinating Scripture:

Revelation 22:17(KJV): And the SPIRIT and the bride say, Come. And let him that heareth say, Come. And let him that is athirst come. And whosoever will, let him take the water of life freely.

Deuteronomy 32:39 (KJV): See now that I, even I, am HE, and there is no god with ME: I kill, and I make alive; I wound, and I heal: neither is there any that can deliver out of MY Hand.

Isaiah 46:9-11 (KJV): 9 Remember the former things of old: for I am GOD, and there is none else; I am GOD, and there is none like ME, 10 Declaring the end from the beginning, and from ancient times the things that are not yet done, saying, MY Counsel shall stand, and I will do all MY Pleasure: 11 Calling a ravenous bird from the east, the man that executeth MY Counsel from a far country: yea, I have spoken it, I will also bring it to pass; I have purposed it, I will also do it.

Job 12:10 (KJV): In WHOSE Hand is the soul of every living thing, and the breath of ALL mankind.

34. I WANT TO SUP WITH A BRIDE WHO ENJOYS MY COMPANY AND NOT A HARLOT WHO LOVES THE WORLD MORE THAN ME

(Words Received from Our LORD by Susan, February 2, 2014)

I do have Words I want to give you. This is for the people:

Children it is your GOD Speaking:

I want to make you aware of something. I am coming soon. Children you must understand something: I am not coming back for a dead church. What do I mean by dead? I mean the lukewarm church. The lukewarm are dead in their sin. They are already dead and buried if they don't renew themselves in MY Blood Covering. Their sins are not covered by anything if they have a wrong relationship with ME. If they are not pursuing ME with all their heart, soul, mind, and strength then they are in dire straits.

The lukewarm who see themselves as in good standing with ME, their GOD, have been fooled by the devil and they cannot be saved apart from ME. I am the ONE WHO can save them, but they are foolish and lost. If you do not wake up and come into MY Blood Covering quickly, you may live to regret it as no one knows the exact hour or day of their demise…

There is danger for the lukewarm who believe confidently they are right with ME. On that day, I will hear, "LORD, LORD…" but their pleas will be insufficient to change MY Mind regarding their lukewarm behavior. I will not take lightly to their ongoing life of disregard for their GOD. I require intimacy; knowing GOD; relationship; and MY lukewarm will have no part in it—they want to touch the HOLY and dispense with the requirements I have set before them to lead HOLY lives. It is too easy to look and live like the world rather than pursuing GOD from a heart that is pure and surrendered.

O' Woe to MY lukewarm. They must come to ME in humble submission. I want to sup with a bride who enjoys MY Company and not a harlot who loves the world more than ME. This is the world, and I cannot tolerate it any longer from MY children. The disappointment has come to MY Throne. I am saddened to the core, over MY lost lukewarm who are returning to follow the world instead of their SAVIOR. Soon they will see the cost and price of their decisions to live a lukewarm lifestyle. Come away O' dead church— wash your garments—follow your GOD down the path that is narrow. Release your grip on the world. This is the time and not later.

I am GOD: RULER over the lukewarm and the bride

Coordinating Scripture:

Matthew 7:21-23 (KJV): 21 Not everyone that saith unto ME, LORD, LORD, shall enter into the Kingdom of Heaven; but he that doeth the Will of MY FATHER which is in Heaven. 22 Many will say to ME in that day, LORD, LORD, have we not prophesied in THY Name? And in THY Name have cast out devils? And in THY Name done many wonderful works? 23 And then will I profess unto them, I never knew you: depart from ME, ye that work iniquity.

Revelation 3:16 (KJV): So then because thou art lukewarm, and neither cold nor hot, I will spue thee out of MY Mouth.

Mark 12:30 (KJV): And thou shalt love the LORD thy GOD with all thy heart, and with all thy soul, and with all thy mind, and with all thy strength: this is the first Commandment.

Revelation 3:18 (KJV): I counsel thee to buy of ME gold tried in the fire, that thou mayest be rich; and white raiment, that thou mayest be clothed, and that the shame of thy nakedness do not appear; and anoint thine eyes with eyesalve, that thou mayest see.

James 5:2 (KJV): Your riches are corrupted, and your garments are motheaten.

Revelation 16:15 (KJV): Behold, I come as a thief. Blessed is he that watcheth, and keepeth his garments, lest he walk naked, and they see his shame.

35. SURRENDER YOUR ALL TO CHRIST

Dear Followers of CHRIST:

When someone makes the choice to surrender their ALL to the LORD CHRIST accepting HIS sacrifice on the cross for salvation, submitting to the will of GOD, and is filled with the HOLY SPIRIT (receiving a full oil lamp) then they are made perfect in GOD's Eyes although they are still occupying a cursed body. GOD accounts the choice made by the person to surrender to GOD's Will as choosing "perfectly" moving them into GOD's PERFECT WILL for their life.

It is a lot like this: when you make the perfect choice FOR GOD— then you immediately become part of the family of GOD: Ephesians 3:14-15 (KJV):14 For this cause I bow my knees unto the FATHER of our LORD JESUS CHRIST, 15 Of WHOM the whole FAMILY in heaven and earth is named,

So when you move into the royal house of GOD by choosing to live for GOD—you live inside HIS Perfection—BUT since you come as you are (imperfect) you are still being sanctified by the LORD. While you live in the royal house and enjoy all the comforts of the royal house (Salvation through CHRIST, filling of the HOLY SPIRIT, fruits of the SPIRIT for example), you will still be instructed to clean up by the washing of the Word and to come apart from the world (culture/world views that run against CHRIST), and to adopt the image of CHRIST all the while you are living inside the royal house of GOD. This is the beautiful image the HOLY SPIRIT gave me of the scripture Hebrews 10:14 (KJV): For by one offering HE hath perfected forever them that are sanctified.

Please note: Below are two letters from the LORD; several new links for The LORD's End Times Prophecy Conference and other special programs; as well as some new dream/vision updates. We had something miraculous happen at the recent conference (among many things that happened). I (Susan) was at the conference lunch Sat. and chose to sit with Cher Cheng Xiong and his wife and daughter who had driven through a winter storm to come to the conference. Cher Cheng told me all about his encounters with CHRIST and seeing hell and it was amazing. So I asked him would he be willing to share his amazing testimony with the people and he was glad to. It was really powerful and the people were really moved—he was a totally unexpected guest speaker. You can hear his powerful testimony at the end of my "Intimacy with GOD" presentation included in the link here below.

36. ALL IS ABOUT CHOICES—CHOOSING LIFE WITH ME OR DEATH WITH MY ENEMY

(Words Received from Our LORD by Susan, February 12, 2014)

Susan this is your GOD—I am ready to give you Words

I am the GOD of the Heavens—I am the GOD of the earth—I am about to remove MY bride from the earth—to take her out to safety—to allow her to be freed from the world. The world is full of evil—evil intent. Evil MY children is all that goes against ME, GOD. Rebellion is that which goes against MY Will and MY Ways. I have set before you a choice. I have given you opportunity to choose the direction you want to move in: whether it is with MY enemy or with ME, your MAKER.

If you choose with MY enemy, you will be lost for eternity in hell. If you choose for ME, then you may come out with ME, when I come to get MY bride—MY true church. This is who I will be coming back to get—to receive unto MYSELF—to pull to safety. Al I the others who choose against ME will remain behind and one of two things will happen to those who remain behind: they will either be left to face the wrath of MY enemy and the wrath of GOD simultaneously while alive on the earth or they will be caught up in the sudden destruction that will come upon the earth immediately following the removal of the church—the bride. It is that simple. Those who are not pulled free when I come to rescue MY own and are caught in sudden destruction will be caught up into eternal damnation apart from the LIVING GOD.

This is serious MY children. You must sober yourselves and come to the realization that the world is about to be overrun by horror and I will be removing the bride and the earth will not look the same. Already the earth is beginning to cave in on itself through gross evil taking over the four corners of the globe. Come to your senses— see your HUMBLE GOD. I gave all for you—I bled on a cross of death for MY people so that they might live with ME for eternity. I gave compassionately and now you must choose WHO you want to follow and what you want to believe.

Do you want to believe MY Words—the Words of MY Book that I have given for you to wash yourself in? This is the work of MY SPIRIT to provide you with access to MY Words, MY Truth, MY Ways. Do you want to get to know ME in humble intimacy through prayer, through seeking ME, through worship and time spent together?

You must choose. There are choices to make. Time spent pursuing the world or time spent pursuing your GOD and knowing ME and MY ways. ALL is about choices—choosing LIFE with ME or death with MY enemy. Submit to ME and live. Run from ME and MY Ways and you will be lost for all eternity. You have freewill to choose but the offer will not always be available, so think this through carefully as your time to choose for ME, your GOD is shortening every day. I love you, but I will not always be so patient with this gross evil world.

This is your GOD: the GOD WHO is Loving, Kind, and LONGSUFFERING

YAHUSHUA HA MASCHIACH

Coordinating Scripture:

Matthew 12:50 (KJV): For whosoever shall do the will of MY FATHER which is in heaven, the same is MY brother, and sister, and mother.

1 Samuel 15:23 (KJV): For rebellion is as the sin of witchcraft, and stubbornness is as iniquity and idolatry. Because thou hast rejected the word of the Lord, he hath also rejected thee from being king.

Joshua 24:15 (KJV): And if it seem evil unto you to serve the Lord, choose you this day whom ye will serve; whether the gods which your fathers served that were on the other side of the flood, or the gods of the Amorites, in whose land ye dwell: but as for me and my house, we will serve the Lord.

1 Thessalonians 5:3 (KJV): For when they shall say, Peace and safety; then sudden destruction cometh upon them, as travail upon a woman with child; and they shall not escape.

1 Thessalonians 5:6 (KJV): Therefore let us not sleep, as do others; but let us watch and be sober.

37. AWAKEN O' LUKEWARM CHURCH

(Words Received from Our LORD by Susan, February 18, 2014)

Yes, I am your GOD and I am ready to give you Words.

My children, this is your GOD, the GOD of Abraham, Isaac, and Jacob.

I am a GOD WHO is dissatisfied. There is a stink and a stench rising up to MY Throne. It is the world under MY Feet, the world that is MY Footstool. I cannot tolerate the stink and stench much longer. Children, you must ready yourselves. Get your garments cleaned up. Wash yourself in the Blood I have given so freely to you. MY Blood is freely available. It is poured out for you to use. It is the Blood that was made available when I died on the cross, Calvary's Cross.

A handsome price was paid, a giant sacrifice from GOD HIMSELF: MY Body torn to pieces by a pack of wolves...evil man motivated by MY enemy to pierce ME...to whip and scourge ME...to tear out MY Beard...to drive nails through MY Feet and Hands.

You must prepare yourselves MY children. I am ready to begin anew. I am ready to bring MY Kingdom about to start the reign and rule of the New Jerusalem with MY lovely bride at MY Side. She pleases ME so much. She has prepared herself and made herself ready. She is looking forward to MY Return. There are no words to describe MY Affection for her. She takes MY Breath away.

I love to watch her. I love to see her and her affection for her GOD: MY sweet church who I love so much, MY bride, MY covenant bride, MY lovely ones who do not become despondent in waiting for MY

Return. I am waiting for the few more who will seek ME: those who really want to be with ME in the next life.

Few have let go so completely of the world as MY true bride. The rest cannot seem to let go to turn their back to the evil world. They will soon have the marriage they are vying for, marriage to an evil world in covenant with MY enemy against ME, their GOD.

Awaken O' lukewarm church. Break free from this repulsive covenant. Tear your hearts away from the love of the world and the enemy. Wash your hands of this evil world. Come away with ME and live free from evil. I am the ONLY ONE WHO can save you from what is coming upon this evil earth. Dark days are soon ahead. Even now it is already becoming so dark, a world that hates GOD. You must run to ME, make your way to ME. I am not a man that I should lie. There are streams of LIVING WATERS if you choose ME. The hour is coming when this choice will not be an easy one, so think this through carefully. Take MY Book and read it: I will guide you. This is an edict from the Throne Room.

This is your GOD,

AUTHOR of Salvation

Coordinating Scripture:

Matthew 5:35 (KJV): Nor by the earth; for it is HIS Footstool: neither by Jerusalem; for it is the city of the great King.

Revelation 19:7 (KJV): Let us be glad and rejoice, and give honour to HIM: for the Marriage of the LAMB is come, and HIS wife hath made herself ready.

Matthew 20:19 (KJV): And shall deliver HIM to the Gentiles to mock, and to scourge, and to crucify HIM: and the third day HE shall rise again.

Psalm 22:16 (KJV): For dogs have compassed ME: the assembly of the wicked have enclosed ME: they pierced MY Hands and MY Feet.

John 7:38 (KJV): He that believeth on ME, as the scripture hath said, out of his belly shall flow rivers of LIVING WATER.

38. SIGNS OF THE END TIMES

Dear Followers of CHRIST:

The Scripture is very clear about the signs of the end times and how everything would converge at once and the events that would come together at one time in history as outlined in the Bible. It is not only the way things would happen and what would happen, but that they would all come at once. This could be the most significant sign of all: even more than all the events you see happening now as detailed in the Bible as events to come and specifically what to look for. Not one or two events foretold, but multiple events occurring simultaneously: earthquakes in diverse places... pestilences... famines... and fearful sights and great signs.

Luke 21:11 (KJV): And great earthquakes shall be in divers places, and famines, and pestilences; and fearful sights and great signs shall there be from heaven.

Men's hearts waxing cold and rumors of wars along with the fulfillment of the Mark of the Beast technology among many other signs all happening, now... The list is long—yet these things are in fact happening just as the Bible indicated hundreds of years ago by prophets like Daniel and our LORD in the New Testament. So, one of the greatest signs that NOW is the time of the return of the LORD for HIS church that the LORD spoke clearly about is the long list of signs COMING TOGETHER during one distinct period of time.

We should stand in awe and cheer that our GOD is SO PRECISE. HE laid it out in detail hundreds of years ago—and hundreds of years later—it is coming together with rapid fire precision. PRAISE THE LORD! GOD is all these things: ACCURATE; RELIABLE; TRUSTWORTHY; TRUE TO HIS WORDS; AND COMING SOON! I am so glad I have a GOD WHO can be counted on. What a comfort in a world that is flaky; unreliable; bleak-looking; and growing ever darker. I am putting my faith in the ANCIENT of days WHO says what HE will do and does it!

With this letter below are links to downloadable materials and radio shows and also attached to this email are several books/documents also.

39. THE EVIL IS CASCADING, OVERFLOWING INTO ALL ASPECTS OF LIFE

(Words Received from Our LORD by Susan, March 29, 2014)

Daughter, I will begin to give you words:

MY children, it is I, your LORD and SAVIOR. The winds are blowing from the east to the west. I am seeing darkness accumulating around the globe—the world that is infested with demons and dark spirits who possess the souls of lost men. Men have given themselves over to darkness against the works of MY SPIRIT. They want to destroy all that I stand for, all that I, GOD represent on earth.

The evil is cascading, overflowing into all aspects of life. Only a few are really entrusted with MY Word, MY Truth—the rest have given themselves over to doctrines of devils. Some seem easier to spot and others not so easy. Many are falling prey to what looks right but leading many astray believing wrongly they are right with ME, but are yet far away. This is the heart of the lukewarm church—lost believers who believe all is well between US, but might as well be practicing gross evil for their lukewarm condition.

Soon, I will be coming to get MY "ready" church—those who are watching, waiting patiently, and no longer enamored with this evil world. The lukewarm church is occupied with the things of the world and makes little or no time for their CREATOR. This is an abomination! It is a lackluster show of affection and I, GOD am slighted, diminished in their true desires which the world has overtaken in their hearts. I know I am low on their list of needs, pursuits, interest. I know the hearts of all men—nothing gets by ME.

Lukewarm: please step out of your tepid condition—seek ME from a heart of fire and zeal to get to know your GOD as your Most Intimate CONFIDANT. Stop trivializing your MAKER, as if I am of no importance and I should only make appearances when you feel it is best: times of crisis and times of holidays. This is a most putrid and foul smell in my nostrils. I cannot honor such lackluster love and your disingenuous feelings for ME. I died a horrible death and bled out in a way that no man should suffer, yet I did this for MY loyal followers and those who would submit to ME with their ALL and desire ME with their FULLEST devotion. All others are useless to

ME in this life because they walk outside the Will of MY FATHER and will be discarded, as I will spit them out.

A fence sitting-Christian, is not on the fence—this Christian is already heading to hell. Only those off the fence with a FULL surrender made to ME, repentant and sorrowful for past sin, forgiving of others, and desiring ME to be their FULL-TIME LORD and MASTER are the ones who will leave earth when I come to rescue MY bride and share with ME eternal life in the Kingdom to come.

If you believe you are on the fence, you are already on your way to hell. Stop playing with fire—time is short and the enemy wants to snatch you away. Many have already gone this way and it is already too late for them as their eternal destiny is now set in stone and they will never have the opportunity you now have to be made right before ME, GOD, so that I accept you before MY FATHER and HIS angels in Heaven. Will this be a moment of terror for you or delight? When you come to face ME, will you have chosen well and will you be with ME for eternity or apart from ME for eternity? Search your souls—decide today which place and with whom you desire to spend eternity. Choose for ME—the LIFEGIVER. I AM HE and there is NO other.

GOD in Heaven:

SAVIOR of ALL—Accepted by few

Coordinating Scripture:

Matthew 24:27-29 (KJV): 27 For as the lightning cometh out of the east, and shineth even unto the west; so shall also the coming of the SON of man be. 28 For wheresoever the carcase is, there will the eagles be gathered together. 29 Immediately after the tribulation of those days shall the sun be darkened, and the moon shall not give her light, and the stars shall fall from heaven, and the powers of the heavens shall be shaken:

Revelation 3:16 (KJV): So then because thou art lukewarm, and neither cold nor hot, I will spue thee out of MY Mouth.

1 Corinthians 10:20 (KJV): But I say, that the things which the Gentiles sacrifice, they sacrifice to devils, and not to GOD: and I would not that ye should have fellowship with devils.

1 Timothy 4:1 (KJV): Now the SPIRIT speaketh expressly, that in the latter times some shall depart from the faith, giving heed to seducing spirits, and doctrines of devils;

Revelation 3:5 (KJV): He that overcometh, the same shall be clothed in white raiment; and I will not blot out his name out of the Book of Life, but I will confess his name before MY FATHER, and before HIS angels.

40. QUESTIONS FOR AND ANSWERS FROM GOD

(Words Received from Our LORD by Susan, March 30, 2014)

Susan's Question: If a person wants to be right with GOD, what is the best way to go about it?

The LORD's Answer: This is what I say: MY children: learn to know your GOD by seeking ME in the secret place—a place you can go to be alone and with your GOD. I long to be with you in your quiet, focused moments—where I am in the forefront of your mind—not hindered by the busy-ness of the day. Seek ME in this way and I can be found. Repent of sin and do it frequently as I am a HOLY GOD and I require purity and holiness. I have made a way for you to find ME—by the blood-bought salvation that I brought through a difficult sacrifice on a hard cross. You can come into MY Presence now because I paid the price for this liberty. Come and get to know ME—I am not far from anyone and I long to know you. The time is short—don't waste it on worldly pursuits, empty and full of sadness is what you will find apart from ME. I offer fullness of life and love everlasting. Come and be close to ME and I will lead you by still waters. This is MY desire for your life. I AM has Spoken.

Psalm 91:1-2 (KJV): He that dwelleth in the secret place of the MOST HIGH shall abide under the Shadow of the ALMIGHTY. 2 I will say of the LORD, HE is my REFUGE and my FORTRESS: my GOD; in HIM will I trust.

Psalm 81:7 (KJV): Thou calledst in trouble, and I delivered thee; I answered thee in the secret place of thunder: I proved thee at the waters of Meribah. Selah.

Psalm 23:2 (KJV): HE maketh me to lie down in green pastures: HE leadeth me beside the still waters.

Matthew 7:23 (KJV): And then will I profess unto them, I NEVER KNEW YOU: depart from me, ye that work iniquity.

Susan's Question: The world is getting very dark—how can we conquer our fears?

The LORD's Answer: Here is the answer: I am capable of handling your fear—put it on MY Shoulder—surrender your fear to ME and allow ME a chance to change your heart. I cannot always change your circumstances because I have plans for people's lives and some things cannot be altered but trust in ME and I can deliver you from feelings of fear and hopelessness even in the worst conditions. MY disciples sang while they were in prison. This stems from the peace of GOD—the same peace is available to you now. Surrender your ALL to ME and your fears and I will show you I am a GOD WHO can be trusted.

James 4:7 (KJV): Submit yourselves therefore to GOD. Resist the devil, and he will flee from you.

Psalm 7:1 (KJV): O LORD my GOD, in THEE do I put my trust: save me from all them that persecute me, and deliver me:

Psalm 56:11 (KJV): In GOD have I put my trust: I will not be afraid what man can do unto me.

Acts 16:25 (KJV): And at midnight Paul and Silas prayed, and sang praises unto GOD: and the prisoners heard them.

Susan's Question: How can we safeguard ourselves spiritually from the influences of the world?

The LORD's Answer: This is what you must do: keep your focus on ME, your GOD. Without this focus, you will fall prey of the works of MY enemy and he comes to steal, kill, and destroy. Focus on your GOD and you will be able to fight the pull of the world. I know the challenges that await you—but I am bigger than all of these, so let ME be the ONE to care for you in all your circumstances. Spend time with ME. Get to know ME as worthy of your knowing. I will lead you to higher ground and draw you away from the influences that distract you from ME. I want a bride whose eyes are only on ME.

John 10:10 (KJV): The thief cometh not, but for to steal, and to kill, and to destroy: I am come that they might have life, and that they might have it more abundantly.

Deuteronomy 4:29 (KJV): But if from thence thou shalt seek the LORD thy GOD, thou shalt find HIM, if thou seek HIM with all thy heart and with all thy soul.

Susan's Question: What can be done to reach out to the most resistant to the Gospel of our family?

The LORD's Answer: If you have someone who does not want MY Message who is close to you—keep your faith no matter what and don't allow them to discourage you. MY children who dislike ME really do not know ME. If people really knew their GOD they would not abandon their ONE TRUE LOVE in exchange for a poor replacement—an empty world and an enemy who wants to see them destroyed. Pray for the people in your lives who resist MY Message. Surrender them to MY Care and I will hear your prayer. Stand in the gap for their soul, pray scriptures over them, and claim healing over their heart and for ME, their GOD, to open them and lead them back to the Truth Everlasting. Persevere and don't allow the enemy to discourage you. I will draw as you pray earnestly for these lost souls. This is MY greatest desire: to partner with MY children to reach the lost and deliver them from eternal hell and loss. Discouragement will come, but victory is also in the grasp of those who speak life, trust, keep their faith, persevere, and hold on to their ONLY HOPE, their GOD.

Ezekiel 22:30 (KJV): And I sought for a man among them, that should make up the hedge, and stand in the gap before ME for the land, that I should not destroy it: but I found none.

Acts 16:14 (KJV): And a certain woman named Lydia, a seller of purple, of the city of Thyatira, which worshipped GOD, heard us: whose heart the LORD opened, that she attended unto the things which were spoken of Paul.

Susan's Question: How can someone overcome the devil?

The LORD's Answer: This is how someone can overcome the devil: It is important to be in MY Will—this is the chief component to combat the enemy. If you walk away from his will—he has no longer jurisdiction over you. You have become MY property, under MY control, MY rule. You no longer belong to the enemy, to do his bidding. I will take control of your life and move you into MY Perfect Ways. This is MY Work to do. Let the people know.

James 4:7 (KJV): SUBMIT yourselves therefore to GOD, resist the devil, and he will flee from you.

41. THE BIBLE DESCRIBES WITH INCREDIBLE DETAIL WHAT IS LITERALLY COMING TO PASS

Dear Followers of CHRIST:

Revelation 14:9-11 (KJV): 9 And the third angel followed them, saying with a loud voice, If any man worship the beast and his image, and receive his mark in his forehead, or in his hand, 10 The same shall drink of the wine of the wrath of GOD, which is poured out without mixture into the cup of his indignation; and he shall be tormented with fire and brimstone in the presence of the holy angels, and in the presence of the LAMB: 11 And the smoke of their torment ascendeth up forever and ever: and they have no rest day nor night, who worship the beast and his image, and whosoever receiveth the mark of his name.

The Bible describes with incredible detail what is literally coming to pass hundreds of years later regarding the "mark of the beast" technology—aka RFID micro-chipping coupled with bar-coding technology. MOST people pass over this detail as if this is well, no big deal and completely forgetting the background of the author who lived hundreds of years ago and would have had no comprehension of such a concept. That makes this all pretty phenomenal and also amazingly...prophetic. This alone makes an extremely convincing argument that the Bible is an accurate document that is prophetic—supporting the view that there IS a GOD WHO knows the future.

Now many—even ministry people—want to convince you that the microchip is not the "mark of the beast" and there is something still coming that will be the actual "mark of the beast." I fear for anyone who spreads this false report around. My question for anyone doing this would be this—what if you are wrong?—What is your next course of action, now that you have prescribed for people to allow themselves to receive a "mark" or chip or microchip tattoo that is identical to the description in the Bible? Can you tell them to take back that which GOD says there is NO ETERNAL SPIRITUAL RECOVERY FROM?

The LORD revealed to me the problem with the RFID micro-chipping going on now. The LORD showed me that the RFID micro-chipping/bar-coding is a kind of attempt for the enemy to be omnipresent via a tracking system that gives detailed knowledge about individuals into the hands of the men. It all seems so positive with a bright future and a wide variety of useful applications—except for one little problem: human beings are surrendering their lives over to imperfect, immoral leadership to rule over them while rejecting GOD as their SOVEREIGN LEADER. Once the choice is made to receive this chip, the individual may wish it were reversible, but GOD will be completely finished with that individual for eternity. I shudder to think of the consequences of such a choice and I am shocked that there are those who are so flippant with their dangerous advice to others that this system is not the one described in the Bible.

Just who told these people this is not the same mark described in the Bible? I challenge these same people to do some research into this technology and see how prolific the technology has become. It does not appear that it will be going away anytime soon—it is only branching out into many areas of use.

So many have already chosen to receive this man-made GOD-replacing technology for a variety of reasons: security; tracking people; healthcare; medical records; personal identification; etc. But the bride of CHRIST is given the ability to see right through this plan of disaster of mankind giving their life over to the enemy. Here are some current links to review showing that this technology is not going to go away and is already becoming quite prominent:

http://www.ncbi.nlm.nih.gov/pmc/articles/PMC1618368/

http://www.spacedaily.com/news/gps-05zzzo.html

http://www.tersosolutions.com/rfid-ensuring-integrity-tissue-medical-devices/

http://www.gpsdaily.com/reports/RFID_Technology_Keeps_Track_Of_School_Bus_Riders_999.html

http://dangerousthings.com/shop/xemi-em4200-2x12mm-injection-kit/

http://rfidtoys.net/index.asp

http://rfidtoys.net/forum/forum_posts.asp?TID=1189&title=some-questions-about-my-implant

http://rfidtoys.net/forum/forum_topics.asp?FID=22&title=rfid-implantation

http://www.fda.gov/Radiation-EmittingProducts/RadiationSafety/ElectromagneticCompatibilityEMC/ucm116647.htm

http://www.biomedical-engineering-online.com/content/12/1/71

With this letter below are links to downloadable materials and radio shows and also attached to this email are several books/documents also.

42. COME AND BE PART OF AN ETERNAL RELATIONSHIP WITH YOUR GOD

(Words Received from Our LORD by Susan, April 13, 2014)

I will begin to give you a letter:

Dear children, It is I, your GOD. I am writing you through this daughter, she is my end time warrior. I am coming and I have wings on MY Feet. I am coming in close and the world is about to see destruction.

The enemy wants to destroy you all. He has plotted and planned against you. His plan Is to annihilate you. He wants nothing better than to destroy you completely. He wants to see you suffer in torment for all of eternity.

The enemy has no love for mankind. He would destroy you all, except for my blood-bought salvation. This was the plan that I had, to counter the evil works of the enemy. The enemy was not looking for a GOD WHO would suffer for HIS lost children. It was not something the enemy would imagine that it was something I, GOD, would do to save those who would come after ME, who would choose for ME, their SAVIOR.

This was not a plan the enemy ever saw coming. I have provided a way for MY lost children. This was MINE to give and I gave it. I GAVE ALL. I gave in FULL measure. I suffered immensely.

The enemy did not know that I, GOD, would lower MYSELF to the level I did for the many lost souls the enemy planned to destroy. But MY Work on the cross vanquished the evil plan of MY opponent and today, you have a way of relief from the cruel ending MY enemy had planned for you.

This was MY Gift for ALL mankind: to save anyone who wanted to be saved, anyone who wanted to be free from the evil of MY enemy. Now, you must choose: will you receive this great blessing of freedom of the enemy and his evil grip on your life? Will you walk on the straight and narrow path with ME to freedom?

I am coming back soon to retrieve MY true church, MY loyal and faithful: "the bride of CHRIST."

She is stunning, and beautiful, and takes my breath away. She leaves ME breathless. I am anxious to sweep her off her feet and carry her out of this ugly world. This is MY deepest desire. I stand ready and I await MY FATHER'S signal.

All heaven is waiting for the arrival of the bride into the Heavenlies. Will you be coming? The choice is yours to make. Repent this day, surrender your all to ME. I am asking you for your hand in marriage. Come and be part of an Eternal Relationship with your GOD. Lay your life down at MY Feet. The time is now. So many are dying and already going by way of the enemy into eternal damnation. I did not lower MYSELF down to lose you. So choose for ME while there is still left time.

These Words are for you to consider. I await your answer to MY Proposal. Amen.

Coordinating Scripture:

2 Samuel 22:11 (KJV): And HE rode upon a cherub, and did fly: and HE was seen upon the wings of the wind.

John 10:10 (KJV): The thief cometh not, but for to steal, and to kill, and to destroy: I am come that they might have life, and that they might have it more abundantly.

Matthew 7:14 (KJV): Because strait is the gate, and narrow is the way, which leadeth unto life, and few there be that find it.

1 Corinthians 15:52 (KJV): In a moment, in the twinkling of an eye, at the last trump: for the trumpet shall sound, and the dead shall be raised incorruptible, and we shall be changed.

Song of Solomon 4:9 (KJV): Thou hast ravished my heart, my sister, my spouse; thou hast ravished my heart with one of thine eyes, with one chain of thy neck.

43. QUESTIONS FOR AND ANSWERS FROM GOD - PART III

(Words Received from Our LORD by Susan, April 19, 2014)

Susan's Question: What should a daily walk with GOD look like?

The LORD's Answer: Susan, this is what I expect from MY children: I ask for a daily surrender, time focused on ME all through the day. This will require decisions—making choices—giving up worldly pursuits in exchange for time spent with ME. I am WORTHY. I created you…I died for you a horrible death. I am ready to come for MY bride. I need the allegiance of MY children.

Matthew 6:24 (KJV): No man can serve two masters: for either he will hate the one, and love the other; or else he will hold to the one, and despise the other. Ye cannot serve GOD and mammon.

Susan's Question: Who is lukewarm and why?

The LORD's Answer: The lukewarm church does not consider pursuing ME daily as worthwhile. They only want ME on their time schedule, on their terms. Daily surrender does not coincide with their plans: their plans for the present or for the future. I am not part of their future planning and if I were, they would be surrendered to MY Will and watching for MY Return DAILY, instead they pursue the things of the world and pin their hopes on the things of man. They will be sorrowful when they are left behind at MY Coming…

Matthew 12:50 (KJV): For whosoever shall do the Will of MY FATHER which is in heaven, the same is MY brother, and sister, and mother.

Psalm 20:7: Some trust in chariots, and some in horses: but we will remember the Name of the LORD our GOD.

Isaiah 31:1: Woe to them that go down to Egypt for help; and stay on horses, and trust in chariots, because they are many; and in horsemen, because they are very strong; but they look not unto the HOLY ONE of Israel, neither seek the LORD!

Isaiah 36:9: How then wilt thou turn away the face of one captain of the least of my master's servants, and put thy trust on Egypt for chariots and for horsemen?

Susan's Question: Why is the bride only a remnant of the population?

The LORD's Answer: MY bride walks a very narrow path as MY Word describes. Some people find this hard to believe, but the coming of the SON of man will be just like the days of Noah. Very few were found watching when the flood came and very few will be found watching when I return. Watching is not a suggestion; it is a requirement for your removal when I bring MY church out. If MY people are not found watching when I return, they will be left behind to face a dark world or worse: sudden destruction.

135

Matthew 7:13-14 (KJV): Enter ye in at the strait gate: for wide is the gate, and broad is the way, that leadeth to destruction, and many there be which go in there at: 14 Because strait is the gate, and narrow is the way, which leadeth unto life, and few there be that find it.

Matthew 24:37-39 (KJV): 37 But as the days of Noah were, so shall also the coming of the SON of man be. 38 For as in the days that were before the flood they were eating and drinking, marrying and giving in marriage, until the day that Noah entered into the ark, 39 And knew not until the flood came, and took them all away; so shall also the Coming of the SON of man be.

Susan's Question: LORD, what do you consider "watching?"

The LORD's Answer: This is MY definition of "watching": Someone who sits on the edge of their seat in anticipation of MY Return. Someone who has their eyes fixed on ME: their LORD and SAVIOR. Someone who reads MY Word, seeks ME at every turn, and watches how MY Word lines up with the events going on in the world. Those who seek MY SPIRIT for HIS Guidance will know the hour they are living in. They will be ready and their lamp will be fully lit. These are MY ready children, MY church, MY bride…

1 Thessalonians 5:1-6 (KJV): 5 But of the times and the seasons, brethren, ye have no need that I write unto you. 2 For yourselves know perfectly that the day of the LORD so cometh as a thief in the night. 3 For when they shall say, Peace and safety; then sudden destruction cometh upon them, as travail upon a woman with child; and they shall not escape. 4 But ye, brethren, are not in darkness, that that day should overtake you as a thief. 5 Ye are all the children of light, and the children of the day: we are not of the night, nor of

darkness. 6 Therefore let us not sleep, as do others; but let us WATCH and be sober.

Addendum: Donna McDonald prayed at my request (Susan) over these questions and this is what she also heard from the LORD: I have prayed over these Words and this is what the LORD has to say about the questions above:

Q1: About surrendering daily. It is simple. If you do as I say you will find yourself with ME for eternity. If you do not, you won't. You will be destined to the eternal pit. It is your choice, you decide. Amen.

Q2: The lukewarm church puts ME on their time schedule. MY bride (that will be raptured) puts MY time schedule as their first priority. The bride will be raptured, the lukewarm church will not, you decide. Amen

Q3: The lukewarm are going downhill rapidly on skates: not watching where they are going. MY bride will be raptured and they are walking Hand-in-hand with ME on a very narrow road. The lukewarm will be left behind for torture and beheading or worse: sudden death and hell. You decide where you want to go. Amen.

Q4: MY bride is watching with binoculars, microscopes, and telescopes for MY Return. She pursues ME at every chance and at every corner. The lukewarm church could care less and they will pay dearly for their lack of concern. Amen.

This is the conclusion of MY explanation of these Words given to MY daughter, Susan Davis. Put this out, daughters, as a confirmation of this set of questions for your GOD. Amen.

44. RIGHT-STANDING WITH GOD

(Words given by the LORD to Donna McDonald, April 20, 2014)

Dear Followers of CHRIST:

One day I asked the LORD how can people who turn to HIM now stack up against people who have been following HIM for 30 years? Where do these people stand who are brand new Christians with GOD? The LORD then gave me the most amazing answer that truly demonstrates the great heart of GOD.

The LORD told me that if someone turns their life over to HIM and truly surrenders their ALL, repents of their sin, asking for the fullness of the HOLY SPIRIT in their life and from that day forward, and continues to move daily toward GOD then they are in right-standing with GOD regardless of their young status as disciples. Ephesians 5:8 (KJV): For ye were sometimes darkness, but now are ye light in the LORD: walk as children of light:

But on the other hand, if someone who has been following the LORD for 30 years, studying the Bible and then were to turn away back into the darkness, they will be lost despite their 30 years of devotion to GOD. Hebrews 6:6 (KJV): If they shall fall away, to renew them again unto repentance; seeing they crucify to themselves the SON of GOD afresh, and put HIM to an open shame.

The new Christian, although lacking in study and knowledge, who surrenders fully to CHRIST, receives Salvation through the Blood of CHRIST is made new and considered righteous in GOD's Eyes. This is because the new convert has chosen "perfectly" when choosing CHRIST as their Savior and to be in the Will of the FATHER and to be filled daily with the HOLY SPIRIT. And once the individual steps into the Will of the FATHER because he has chosen to, the HOLY SPIRIT will lead that person down the narrow path because the individual is now on GOD's "watch" and CHRIST is then the AUTHOR and FINISHER of the person's eternal outcome. Praise the LORD—CHRIST's Yoke is easy:

Matthew 11:29 (KJV): Take MY Yoke upon you, and learn of ME; for I am meek and lowly in heart: and ye shall find rest unto your souls.

45. EACH DAY APART FROM MY WILL FOR YOUR LIFE IS TIME SPENT IN THE KINGDOM OF DARKNESS...

(Words Received from Our LORD by Susan, April 27, 2014)

Susan, my daughter, I want to give you new Words. These are important Words.

Children, it is I, your GOD, there is shifting like sand. The world is moving to evil, all is growing evil. Only a few adhere to MY Words. Only a few focus on what I have to say, who want to walk with ME every day. Very few are sensitive to MY SPIRIT and pursue the filling of MY SPIRIT. There is a depravity of Truth, MY Truth, MY Word. Very few pursue what is pure, Holy, through the Words found in MY Book, MY Holy Book. The people are not interested in their GOD, their SAVIOR, LORD, and MASTER. The world is collapsing under the weight of its sin--its own sin. It is crumbling and coming apart under the weight of evil, evil that is everywhere. There is only one place that is safe--in MY Arms, surrendered, submitted to MY Will, repentant, and seeking after ME with a child-like faith with a heart that pursues GOD as the ONLY HOPE...the ONLY SHELTER...the ONLY SOLUTION...the ONLY RELIEF to a world dying and full of corruption.

Children, you must come alive, come away. See your GOD as your ONLY HOPE, the ONLY WAY, The NARROW PATH to freedom. There is no other road. All other roads lead to destruction. All other roads are paved with traps, holes, and road blocks placed in your way by MY enemy to destroy you. Surrender to ME and make your way back to the Narrow Road. All other routes are sure destinations to hell and your destruction. These Words are for your benefit, to guide you, lead you, to bring you back to safety.

There is no hope in this dying world except with a relationship with ME, your LORD and SAVIOR. Drop the world, stop holding hands with evil, the evil that surrounds you. You must be set apart. There is no other way.

You must pull away from the world. Only I can enable you to do this. Only I have what you need to pull yourself free from the sin that besets you and keeps you in its grip. It is only by MY SPIRIT that you can accomplish what you need to be set free from the pull of sin and the lure of the world.

Lay your life down. Surrender your ALL. Repent for the sin you commit daily. This is the only way. Acknowledge the price I paid to cover your life of sin, the things you have done against ME, your CREATOR. I will receive you and give you a clean heart, clean robes. You must be willing. Only you can do this, no one else can do this for you.

Turn back to your GOD. I will purify you, clean you up, put a spirit of right-thinking within you, MY SPIRIT. HE will guide you, lead you in MY Perfect Will for your life.

Don't tarry. Each day apart from My Will for your life is time spent in the kingdom of darkness apart from the LOVER of your soul, bringing destruction into your path. Exchange your heart of stone for a heart of flesh. Now is the hour of your deliverance if you accept MY Offer. Receive MY Offer of MY Blood-Covering over your sin, your life of sin against your GOD. There is no other way to blot out your sin and the evil that comes between us and will separate us for eternity.

There is only a brief time before the world will slide into total depravity, into the hands of the enemy. Are you coming out with ME when I retrieve MY bride or staying behind to face the worst?

Salvation is MY Offer. Come and redeem your soul.

I Am the GOD worth knowing, YAHUSHUA

John 12:40 (KJV): He hath blinded their eyes, and hardened their heart; that they should not see with their eyes, nor understand with their heart, and be converted, and I should heal them.

2 Corinthians 4:4 (KJV): In whom the god of this world hath blinded the minds of them which believe not, lest the light of the glorious gospel of CHRIST, WHO is the Image of GOD, should shine unto them.

Matthew 7:13-14 (KJV): 13 Enter ye in at the strait gate: for wide is the gate, and broad is the way, that leadeth to destruction, and many there be which go in thereat: 14 Because strait is the gate, and narrow is the way, which leadeth unto life, and few there be that find it.

Ephesians 5:25-27 (KJV): 25 Husbands, love your wives, even as CHRIST also loved the church, and gave HIMSELF for it; 26 That HE might sanctify and cleanse it with the washing of water by the Word, 27 That HE might present it to HIMSELF a glorious church, not having spot, or wrinkle, or any such thing; but that it should be holy and without blemish.

46. QUESTIONS FOR AND ANSWERS FROM GOD - PART IV

(Words Received from Our LORD by Susan, May 4, 2014)

Susan's Question: How can someone conquer habitual sin?

The LORD's Answer: This is how MY children, can conquer their sin: They need to surrender their ALL to ME, not just their sin, but their whole being: spirit, body, soul, and allow MY SPIRIT to consume them, take them over, renew them, and change their hearts from hearts of stone into hearts of flesh. Any other route to fight off sin will lead to frustration and the penalty of sin is death apart from MY forgiveness. Seek ME and you will find ME. Many men have found forgiveness and relief from long-held sin by the Power of MY HOLY SPIRIT. Turn to ME for relief from sin.

Romans 12:2 (KJV): And be not conformed to this world: but be ye transformed by the renewing of your mind, that ye may prove what is that good, and acceptable, and perfect, Will of GOD.

Titus 3:5 (KJV): Not by works of righteousness which we have done, but according to HIS mercy HE saved us, by the washing of regeneration, and renewing of the HOLY GHOST;

1 John 5:18 (KJV): We know that whosoever is born of GOD sinneth not; but he that is begotten of GOD keepeth himself, and that wicked one toucheth him not.

Romans 8:1-11 (KJV): 8 There is therefore now no condemnation to them which are in CHRIST JESUS, who walk not after the flesh, but after the SPIRIT. 2 For the law of the SPIRIT of life in CHRIST JESUS hath made me free from the law of sin and death. 3 For what the law could not do, in that it was weak through the flesh, GOD sending HIS Own SON in the likeness of sinful flesh, and for sin, condemned sin in the flesh: 4 That the righteousness of the law might be fulfilled in us, who walk not after the flesh, but after the SPIRIT.

Susan's Question: How can someone be of GOD and still living in this world?

The LORD's Answer: How to live in the world and to not be of the world is about semantics--are you part of the world, choosing for the things of the world, what men say is right? Or are you living among men in the world, but basing your decisions on what I, GOD, say is right? You have choices to make when you live in this world. You can do things by the way men around you choose to live or you can pursue a life surrendered to ME, your GOD and live by MY precepts and rules outlined clearly in MY Word lived out by the guidance of MY HOLY SPIRIT. This is the difference of living in the world and being of the world.

1 John 2:16 (KJV): For all that is in the world, the lust of the flesh, and the lust of the eyes, and the pride of life, is not of the FATHER, but is of the world.

Psalm 119:128 (KJV): Therefore I esteem all THY precepts concerning all things to be right; and I hate every false way.

Philippians 2:15 (KJV): That ye may be blameless and harmless, the sons of GOD, without rebuke, in the midst of a crooked and perverse nation, among whom ye shine as lights in the world;

Colossians 2:8 (KJV): Beware lest any man spoil you through philosophy and vain deceit, after the tradition of men, after the rudiments of the world, and not after CHRIST.

Susan's Question: How can a person live inside YOUR Will on a daily basis?

The LORD's Answer: This is what I require: a FULL surrender of the WHOLE life over to MY complete Will, not a partial surrender. Partial, meaning some of the time or when the individual feels moved to do what seems right. A full surrender to MY Will is a hunger, thirst to walk away from MY enemy into MY Ways, Truth, and to fully desire ME to possess your life: mind, body, soul, spirit-- complete surrender. You must give ME permission to run your life as I see fit to take you down paths of righteousness, to move you into MY future plan for your life, and to deal with you as I see fit, trusting in MY total consumption of your being into MY SPIRIT-led Ways.

A partial surrender will lead you into double-mindedness, confusion, and ultimately walking outside MY Will. This is the walk of many, the lukewarm, the lost. MY Way is an ALL or nothing proposition. Choose today whom you will serve.

Matthew 5:6 (KJV): Blessed are they which do hunger and thirst after righteousness: for they shall be filled.

Revelation 3:16 (KJV): So then because thou art lukewarm, and neither cold nor hot, I will spue thee out of MY Mouth.

James 1:8 (KJV): A double-minded man is unstable in all his ways.

James 4:8 (KJV): Draw nigh to GOD, and HE will draw nigh to you. Cleanse your hands, ye sinners; and purify your hearts, ye double-minded.

Joshua 24:15 (KJV): And if it seem evil unto you to serve the LORD, choose you this day whom ye will serve; whether the gods which your fathers served that were on the other side of the flood, or the gods of the Amorites, in whose land ye dwell: but as for me and my house, we will serve the LORD.

Susan's Question: How can someone know if they are truly a believer or an unbeliever?

The LORD's Answer: Daughter, even the demons believe there is a GOD. MY children must really pursue ME with all their hearts. I want total devotion. I want FULL surrender. I want a relationship, not a part-time, distant friendship: one that is called up when it seems necessary in crisis or times of hardship. Many of MY children know ME not. They think they know ME because of their occasional rote worship and habitual visits to their churches and places of worship. This does not represent intimacy. Is a husband faithful if he only talks to his wife once or twice a week? I am not interested in a short-term relationship. I want to be above all others in your life. This is what I require. You are not fit for MY Kingdom if you place ME below parents, spouse, and children. Does MY Word not speak this? Soon I am coming back for a church that is fully committed to ME. All others will be left behind. These are MY terms, this is what I require for entrance into MY Kingdom.

Luke 9:62 (KJV): And JESUS said unto him, No man, having put his hand to the plough, and looking back, is fit for the Kingdom of GOD.

Luke 14:26 (KJV): If any man come to ME, and hate not his father, and mother, and wife, and children, and brethren, and sisters, yea, and his own life also, HE cannot be MY disciple.

Dear Followers of CHRIST:

It has been a little while since a letter has gone out, but it is not because there isn't anything going on… So I just want to update you on the latest happenings…

I put everything on hold for a week so that I could focus on reading and editing Othusitse Mmusi's New Book: "Revelation of Heaven and Hell." Othusitse is a young man from Botswana and I describe him as a "young Isaiah" because the things the LORD is revealing to him about heaven, hell, and the LORD's Soon Coming is really just phenomenal.

How did I get to know Othusitse and come to help with his book project since I live in Indiana and he lives in Botswana? Well it can only be explained because we work for the same Boss: The HOLY SPIRIT. I highly recommend that you take time to read Othusitse's amazing book (FREE downloadable EBook) "Revelation of Heaven and Hell" and follow up with our other Free Books (by Susan Davis) including:

"Marriage Supper of the LAMB";

"Bride of CHRIST: Prepare Now";

"Left Behind After the Rapture"; and

"Rapture and Tribulation."

All books are FREE and available with links below or by email at kidsmkg@sbclgobal.net I am including a Letter from the LORD also below excerpted from Othusitse's new book. Here is the FREE Ebook Download:

47. EVERY DAY YOU WALK APART FROM ME AS YOUR LORD AND MASTER IS A DAY WASTED WITH MY ENEMY

(Words Received from Our LORD by Susan, May 14, 2014)

I am ready to give thee Words:

Children, it is I, your LORD. There is a great bewilderment over the world. Changes are coming about, great moves towards evil. MY SPIRIT is also on the move. HE is enlightening the hearts of many to the times you are living in. You are living in dark times. MY SPIRIT is showing HIMSELF Great. HE is fulfilling MY WORD that HE would be utterly poured out to warn the people of the dark days ahead. HE is coming through young and old alike: through dreams, visions, and prophetic utterances. All these are coming as warnings to prepare, to be ready, and to stand guard as MY enemy wants to destroy you and keep you from MY rescue. This is his greatest desire, to prolong your stay and to keep you from MY Glorious Coming to rescue MY bride. He is bent on destruction, your destruction. You must resist him. You must fight against him. Put on your armor, your armor of Power, the armor that MY HOLY SPIRIT gives. Ask for it and you shall receive it.

Surrender your ALL to ME. I want ALL your soul, mind, spirit, and body with a commitment to follow ME as your LORD and SAVIOR, MASTER, REDEEMER. I need a FULL commitment, nothing less will do. Partial commitment is no commitment and leaves you wide

148

open for MY enemy to enter into your heart and leaves you vulnerable to destruction. You cannot fight this enemy on your own. You need the FULL embodiment of MY SPIRIT indwelling your spirit to take on this evil force, MY foe. Without giant doses of MY Word with the guidance of MY SPIRIT and MY FORGIVENESS for your repentant sin daily, your efforts to fight off sin and to clean up your robes will be useless. O' you can have a form of godliness with a partial commitment, a lukewarm surrender, but you will lack the Power thereof and you will ultimately lose your salvation and be cast away into hell.

Make up your mind to enter into MY Peace, MY Salvation, Purity, Wholeness. Discard the world you cling to heartily and surrender your ALL to MY Will, MY Leadership, My Guidance, and I will lead you out on the narrow path and make you ready for MY Coming. There is no other way. I AM a GOD of complete Truth, not lies and half truths. Study MY Word and show yourself approved. Come to know the Truth by the leading by MY SPIRIT. Time is wasting for you.

Every day you walk apart from ME as your LORD and MASTER is a day wasted with MY enemy outside of MY Will for your life. MY Patience for this evil world will soon be stifled at the moment of MY Coming. Be ready, TAKE ACTION!

This is The LORD of the universe,

CHRIST The SAVIOR

Coordinating Scripture:

Joel 2:28 (KJV): And it shall come to pass afterward, that I will pour out MY SPIRIT upon all flesh; and your sons and your daughters shall prophesy, your old men shall dream dreams, your young men shall see visions:

Acts 2:17 (KJV): And it shall come to pass in the last days, saith GOD, I will pour out of MY SPIRIT upon all flesh: and your sons and your daughters shall prophesy, and your young men shall see visions, and your old men shall dream dreams:

Acts 2:18 (KJV): And on MY servants and on MY handmaidens I will pour out in those days of MY SPIRIT; and they shall prophesy:

Ephesians 6:10-18 (KJV): 10 Finally, my brethren, be strong in the LORD, and in the Power of HIS Might. 11 Put on the whole armour of GOD, that ye may be able to stand against the wiles of the devil. 12 For we wrestle not against flesh and blood, but against principalities, against powers, against the rulers of the darkness of this world, against spiritual wickedness in high places. 13 Wherefore take unto you the whole armour of GOD, that ye may be able to withstand in the evil day, and having done all, to stand. 14 Stand therefore, having your loins girt about with Truth, and having on the breastplate of righteousness; 15 And your feet shod with the preparation of the gospel of peace; 16 Above all, taking the shield of faith, wherewith ye shall be able to quench all the fiery darts of the wicked. 17 And take the helmet of salvation, and the sword of the SPIRIT, which is the Word of GOD: 18 Praying always with all prayer and supplication in the SPIRIT, and watching thereunto with all perseverance and supplication for all saints;

2 Timothy 3:5 (KJV): Having a form of godliness, but denying the power thereof: from such turn away.

48. QUESTIONS FOR AND ANSWERS FROM GOD - PART V

(Words Received from Our LORD by Susan, May 16, 2014)

Susan's Question: What does it mean to be in YOUR Will?

The LORD's Answer: This is the meaning of the question: to be in MY Will you must surrender your ALL to ME, your LORD and SAVIOR, to desire to do things MY Way, to lay down your life, to deny your own self will and future plans, to put ME above all else. This is a decision, a choice to walk away from the will and future plans of MY enemy. You must decide who you want to be for. Do you want your life to belong to ME or MY enemy? I give this freedom to choose. Choosing against ME will have grave consequences. If you choose against ME, you cannot be part of MY Eternal Kingdom. Hell is the alternative to MY Heavenly Kingdom. It is the place for those who choose against ME. It is a place that lacks the goodness of GOD.

Mark 8:34 (KJV): And when HE had called the people unto HIM with HIS disciples also, HE said unto them, Whosoever will come after ME, let him deny himself, and take up his cross, and follow ME.

Susan's Question: How does one proceed with their life when they surrender to YOUR Will? How can they know what to do?

The LORD's Answer: Daughter, this is when MY surrendered children must learn to trust in ME, their GOD. I can be trusted. They must come to ME throughout the day, as a child would seek a parent. They must pray to be in MY Will through their day and when hard decisions arise, and to allow MY SPIRIT to come into their life to guide and lead them. They must ask for MY SPIRIT to take them over and to lead them to green pastures: right decisions, correct choices, and guidance from Above. I will not lead them astray. There will be trials and tribulations, but MY Hand will guide and deliver like no other hand. A helpless trust in ME, that is what I want from MY children so that I can shine through MY children out into a dark world that runs apart from ME, its MAKER.

Psalm 23:2 (KJV): HE maketh me to lie down in green pastures: HE leadeth me beside the still waters.

Susan's Question: What does it mean to have a full oil lamp as described in the parable of the ten virgins?

The LORD's Answer: Yes, child, let us review that important parable. There were ten virgins all with a lamp: each had a measure of oil. Some had lamps that were half-full and the rest had full oil lamps. Oil is the fuel in a lamp enabling the light to be lit. MY HOLY SPIRIT is like that oil. HE is the Power or Oil within the person. It represents the "focus" on GOD. Some are half-focused and partially lit. While the others are fully-focused and fully-lit. Those who are fully-focused and -lit are fully-watching for MY Return and walking in MY Ways. They shine bright and will be seen when I come back for MY own, MY bride. The others, who are not focused on ME with only half of their lamp filled, will remain behind to face the worst, the left behind foolish virgins.

Matthew 25:1-13: (Parable of the Ten Virgins)

Susan's Question: What are people to do if they already have future plans made after they surrender to your Will?

The LORD's Answer: This is what I want MY people to do. I want them to lay their lives at MY Feet, including their plans then let ME lead, let ME show MY Strength. I will close doors and open doors. I will put things in their heart to do once they give ME permission to take over their lives. I will give them hearts of flesh. They will seek ME to direct their paths and I can be trusted to do it. Only MY children who seek to follow ME find their way to MY narrow path. All others will be lost on the broad way to hell.

2 Corinthians 3:3 (KJV): Forasmuch as ye are manifestly declared to be the epistle of CHRIST ministered by us, written not with ink, but with the SPIRIT of the Living GOD; not in tables of stone, but in fleshy tables of the heart.

Matthew 7:13-14 (KJV): 13 Enter ye in at the strait gate: for wide is the gate, and broad is the way, that leadeth to destruction, and many there be which go in thereat: 14 Because strait is the gate, and narrow is the way, which leadeth unto life, and few there be that find it.

49. WE NEED TO BE "SET APART" FROM THE WORLD

Dear Followers of CHRIST:

The Bible is clear that we need to be "set apart" from the world. Today's Christians are dying from lack of knowledge as it says in Hosea. Oh, the Christians have knowledge: worldly knowledge—but what of the knowledge of GOD? People are building up their earthly 401ks but their Heavenly 401ks are bankrupt.

Today's Christians look identical to the secular and there is no telling them apart. The Christians have embraced the world in the way they dress, the things they are introducing to their homes, and the worldly activities they are participating in.

If I said you shouldn't wear or bring into your home symbols of the occult—you would probably agree with that statement—but many people can't recognize the proliferation of occult symbols now in the world that have become common household symbols. Let's look at these scriptures: one from the Book of Acts in which the Apostle Paul got in trouble with the locals because he challenged their focus on the false deity the goddess Diana, who was nothing more than a mythological god:

Acts 19:26-27 (KJV): 26 Moreover ye see and hear, that not alone at Ephesus, but almost throughout all Asia, this Paul hath persuaded and turned away much people, saying that they be no gods, which are made with hands: 27 So that not only this our craft is in danger to be set at nought; but also that the temple of the great goddess Diana should be despised, and her magnificence should be destroyed, whom all Asia and the world worshippeth.

Another mythological god spoken of in Revelation 2:13 by CHRIST about the church of Pergamos that was at the seat of Satan which was the Altar of Zeus—a chief mythological god of the time:

Revelation 2:13 (KJV): I know thy works, and where thou dwellest, even where Satan's seat is: and thou holdest fast my name, and hast not denied my faith, even in those days wherein Antipas was my faithful martyr, who was slain among you, where Satan dwelleth.

Why are these references significant to the times we are in? Because the people worshipped made-up deity instead of the Living GOD which was all deception driven by Satan who is still driving people to focus their time and pursuits on that which is false away from the Living GOD.

Today there are many products and things that are attached to these symbols of Satan—like the Altar of Zeus as described by CHRIST. Let's look deeper into this matter: items that have their name origins in past mythological gods (remember CHRIST said this was Satanic referencing the Altar of Zeus as the seat of Satan): Starbucks symbol for instance—the mythological water witch—a mermaid (Disney also is big on mermaids); Nike—Nike is the goddess of Victory and Satan's charioteer; Beast Energy Drink—the drink that's symbol is 666 in Hebrew letters the number of Satan; Pandora Radio—Pandora was the first human "created" by the Greek gods in Greek mythology; Dragon Software (Dragon was also the name given to a recent space Shuttle launched)—Dragon, a common symbol of the devil in the Bible; common wind chimes have their origin in the occult from the Hindu deity Ganesha; the 60's popularized peace symbol has its origins in Satanic worship in early centuries; the current rise of interest in tattoos goes against GOD big time and represents rebellion to GOD as the Bible clearly says not to tattoo your body and that this is evil to GOD (although this is an Old Testament teaching—the secular world LOVES to take anything in the Bible GOD despises and use it as a way of making a statement of rebellion against GOD and tattoos certainly applies in this instance); and this list goes on and on from pagan gods of all cultures: Oriental; Indian; Hindu; Islam; Buddhism; American Indian; African paganism; Worship of Mary and other Catholic Saints; ancient paganism such as Egyptian symbols, Mayan symbols, Aztec symbols, and Celtic symbols; New Age symbols; astrology/mediums/psychics; Fantasy such as Dungeons and Dragons and Pokemon; and on and on. CHRIST said the reference to the Greek Altar of Zeus was "the seat of Satan" and you wouldn't wear, bring into your home; and embrace the symbols of Satan you are familiar with like a pentagram that is more commonly associated with the occult. So you have to ask yourself: "Is it time that I stand with GOD against the secular movement that wants desperately to tear down the Living GOD by embracing antichrist symbols and beliefs and avoid dying from lack of knowledge? Pray for the HOLY SPIRIT to show you the things you embrace and have in your home that are offensive to GOD and HE will do it.

Hosea 4:6 (KJV): My people are destroyed for lack of knowledge: because thou hast rejected knowledge, I will also reject thee, that thou shalt be no priest to me: seeing thou hast forgotten the law of thy GOD, I will also forget thy children

50. THOSE WHO FOLLOW MY WAYS ARE LAMPLIGHTERS

(Words Received from Our LORD by Susan, June 8, 2014)

We can begin--Children of the MOST HIGH, I have Words to give you:

Those who follow MY Ways are Lamplighters. They are carriers of Truth. They speak boldly for what is right. They carry Light into a dark world: the Truth, MY Word, the Gospel.

There are very few who want to be Lamplighters: Those who carry the Truth to others. The world is dying in its sin and corruption. Lamplighters bring Truth to the darkest places.

You can be one of MY Light carriers. Surrender your life to ME, your GOD, your SAVIOR. Let ME give you a heart of flesh, let ME take your heart of stone and turn it into flesh. I want to use you in this late hour, but I cannot do that until you are surrendered to MY Will. Outside of MY Will you operate in the will of MY enemy and you accomplish nothing for the Kingdom. You work against MY Ways, MY Truth. Align yourself with MY Will and together and we will accomplish much. Your fruit will abound and your rewards will be great in Heaven.

Choose today what you will do with your life. Will you accomplish great things by the power of MY HOLY SPIRIT in alignment with MY Will or will your life be about destruction and great loss? You decide. The choice is yours to make. Time is short. People die in their sin daily. Join ME in bringing in the harvest of the lost before the "Great Gathering" in the sky.

This is your FATHER and SAVIOR,

BOUNDLESS LOVE

Coordinating Scripture:

Luke 12:35-36 (KJV): 35 Let your loins be girded about, and your lights burning; 36 And ye yourselves like unto men that wait for their LORD, when HE will return from the wedding; that when HE cometh and knocketh, they may open unto HIM immediately.

John 5:33-35 (KJV): 33 Ye sent unto John, and he bare witness unto the truth. 34 But I receive not testimony from man: but these things I say, that ye might be saved. 35 He was a burning and a shining light: and ye were willing for a season to rejoice in his light.

Philippians 2:15 (KJV): That ye may be blameless and harmless, the sons of GOD, without rebuke, in the midst of a crooked and perverse nation, among whom ye shine as lights in the world;

2 Corinthians 3:3 (KJV): Forasmuch as ye are manifestly declared to be the epistle of CHRIST ministered by us, written not with ink, but with the SPIRIT of the Living GOD; not in tables of stone, but in fleshy tables of the heart.

51. YOUR LIFE WAS NOT AN ACCIDENT. I CREATED YOU WITH A GOAL IN MIND.

(Words Received from Our LORD by Susan, June 8, 2014)

I am ready to give you new Words:

I am a GOD WHO is always present. I can be found at any moment. MY children just need to call on MY Name. There is nothing that I cannot change or do. Nothing is impossible for ME, GOD.

You must learn to move in MY Will. You must embrace what is MY Will. How do I do this, you may ask, "How can I be in Your Will?" This is the way to operate in MY Will: I want you to come before ME in humble submission: get before ME and surrender your life to ME. You do not need to know what this means specifically. You just must need to have a strong desire to operate in MY Will, to run in MY Will. This is all I need from you. I need your desire to be in MY Will to want to do what I ask from day to day: to know from this day forward that you are in line with the Will of GOD.

All you need to do is express this to ME daily. Just seek ME for this desire and I will give this to you. Repent of your sin daily and frequently, read MY Word, MY Holy Book. Seek ME in the quiet moments of the day, let me comfort you and be with you all day. Ask ME for a complete filling of MY SPIRIT and HE will come and live in you and lead you. You will never be alone.

This is the desire of MY Heart, for you to walk closely with your LORD, for "your will" to be in align with MY Will, for us to be in one mind and one SPIRIT, for us to be like-minded and then great and wonderful things can be accomplished for MY Kingdom on earth and the Kingdom to come.

Come and share in the Greatness of your GOD. I have many things I want to open up to you. Your life was not an accident. I created you with a goal in mind. Come let us share in the wonders I have in store for you. All this can be yours if you deny yourself of your own will which is the will of MY enemy: the will you operate in outside of MY Will.

Come and be part of the Great Kingdom of GOD and the wonders that await you. This can all be yours. I will not keep anything from you. All that is MINE will be yours. Come and share in the Glory of your GOD, your KING. Time is short, choose for ME. I love you with an "Endless Love." These Words are for you today, cherish and embrace MY Words.

This is your Loving GOD…The KING without end…HOPE EVERLASTING…

Coordinating Scripture:

Luke 1:37 (KJV): For with GOD nothing shall be impossible.

Acts 2:21 (KJV): And it shall come to pass, that whosoever shall call on the Name of the LORD shall be saved.

Matthew 7:21 (KJV): Not everyone that saith unto ME, LORD, LORD, shall enter into the Kingdom of Heaven; but he that doeth the Will of MY FATHER which is in Heaven.

Luke 12:32 (KJV): Fear not, little flock; for it is your FATHER's Good Pleasure to give you the Kingdom.

(Susan said she saw in her spirit right after this letter: I saw a little vision and I saw myself and I saw actual words swirling around me like in a whirlwind.)

52. CHRISTIANS DABBLING IN THE OCCULT

Dear Followers of CHRIST:

Today, I want to talk about a difficult subject: Christians dabbling in the occult.

A couple years ago, my son came home and told me that the English teacher in his Christian high school was recommending the books Twilight: a popular series of stories about vampires. There was a family member who is a self-proclaimed Christian who told me that she and her teenage daughters read the Twilight series and liked them. Other Christians I know have told me, they and their children read both Twilight and Harry Potter books. A friend told me that she even knew of a Pastor of a church in the area who made it known to his congregation that his children were avid readers of Harry Potter and he supported it.

I thought to write on this topic because I rarely now watch TV, but a friend mentioned that they were appalled by all the shows on TV nowadays that are focused on vampire and witchcraft subjects. That's what caused me to write on this topic again. I am even stunned quite honestly at the Christian community's Facebook pages that "like" the Twilight series books and other similar TV/movie/book properties. Not to mention horror movies; shows with dark themes like murder movies and focused on psychics and mediums. The Bible says to think on things of good report: Philippians 4:8(KJV): Finally, brethren, whatsoever things are true, whatsoever things are honest, whatsoever things are just, whatsoever things are pure, whatsoever things are lovely, whatsoever things are of good report; if there be any virtue, and if there be any praise, think on these things.

The LORD once revealed to me that HE did not need "wizards" to tell HIS Story with reference to the books that use wizards and witches to loosely tell the story of CHRIST such as LORD of the RINGS.

I don't think people realize that there is no "fence-sitting" position with CHRIST and you are either WITH HIM or AGAINST HIM in your Christian walk. The Bible says that the world is an enmity to GOD: 1 John 2:15(KJV): Love not the world, neither the things that are in the world. If any man love the world, the love of the FATHER is not in him.

Only those who are focused on the LORD pursuing HIM in holiness will see GOD ACCORDING TO THE BIBLE. So the Christians MUST release their grip on the things like Harry Potter; Twilight; horror movies; vampire shows; books about wizards/witches; psychics/mediums; horoscopes; dark themed films—etc....This is a very serious hour—don't be involved in such things—here is further scripture from both the Old Testament and the New Testament on the LORD's TOTAL DISDAIN for such things:

1 Samuel 15:23(KJV): For rebellion is as the sin of witchcraft, and stubbornness is as iniquity and idolatry. Because thou hast rejected the Word of the LORD, HE hath also rejected thee from being king.

2 Chronicles 33:6(KJV): And he caused his children to pass through the fire in the valley of the son of Hinnom: also he observed times, and used enchantments, and used witchcraft, and dealt with a familiar spirit, and with wizards: he wrought much evil in the Sight of the LORD, to provoke HIM to anger.

Micah 5:12(KJV): And I will cut off witchcrafts out of thine hand; and thou shalt have no more soothsayers:

Galatians 5:19-20 (KJV): Now the works of the flesh are manifest, which are these; Adultery, fornication, uncleanness, lasciviousness, 20 Idolatry, witchcraft, hatred, variance, emulations, wrath, strife, seditions, heresies,

Leviticus 19:31 (KJV): Regard not them that have familiar spirits, neither seek after wizards, to be defiled by them: I am the LORD your GOD.

Leviticus 20:6 (KJV):And the soul that turneth after such as have familiar spirits, and after wizards, to go a whoring after them, I will even set MY Face against that soul, and will cut him off from among his people.

Deuteronomy 18:10-11 (KJV): 10There shall not be found among you any one that maketh his son or his daughter to pass through the fire, or that useth divination, or an observer of times, or an enchanter, or a witch. 11 Or a charmer, or a consulter with familiar spirits, or a wizard, or a necromancer.

Isaiah 19:3 (KJV): And the spirit of Egypt shall fail in the midst thereof; and I will destroy the counsel thereof: and they shall seek to the idols, and to the charmers, and to them that have familiar spirits, and to the wizards.

Revelation 21:8 (KJV): But the fearful, and unbelieving, and the abominable, and murderers, and whoremongers, and sorcerers, and idolaters, and all liars, shall have their part in the lake which burneth with fire and brimstone: which is the second death.

Revelation 22:14-15 (KJV): Blessed are they that do HIS Commandments,that they may have right to the Tree of Life, and may enter in through thegates into the city. 15 For without are dogs, and sorcerers, and whoremongers, and murderers, and idolaters, and whosoever loveth and maketh a lie.

53. THE WORLD MAY BE CRUMBLING, BUT MY BRIDE IS PRESERVED - SHE HAS MY SPIRIT AND SHE IS PRESERVED

(Words Received from Our LORD by Susan, June 21, 2014)

Susan, I am ready to give you Words:

Children, there are dark storm clouds: this is the evil spreading. The world is turning its back to its GOD. The time is dwindling for those who need to get right with ME. Evil is moving swiftly.

Children do you believe the world will go on with evil in charge indefinitely? It can't be—I will not tolerate this indefinitely, although I AM LONGSUFFERING. MY Patience is running thin. Many have already seen the end of MY Patience through disaster or destruction.

I will not abide with evil or strive with evil man forever. I am giving MY Warnings. I have prepared a Place for MY ready bride. She waits patiently as the world falls apart around her. I will not keep her waiting forever. Stay ready MY beautiful bride: keep your focus on your LORD. Keep your eyes fixed on ME.

The world may be crumbling, but MY bride is preserved—she has MY SPIRIT and she is preserved.

Woe to those who try to operate with a partial filling—a half-full oil lamp. You will be left to face destruction when I come to pick up MY bride—MY bride whose lamp overflows with MY HOLY SPIRIT OIL. She is bright and shines forth Truth. She represents her LORD in a dark world: gross evil at every turn. She is a beacon carrying MY Words, MY Gospel with her beautiful feet: pouring out of her lovely mouth.

Children of Light: shine forth; pour out Hope...Light...Truth...MY Gospel...MY Testimony. Tell them of MY Death on a rugged cross: how I bled for the sins of all men. Tell them I AM COMING! Tell them to CALL OUT MY NAME. Seek ME in this dark hour. Tell them I CAN BE FOUND. Tell them I will return to take those who want to be in Glory with ME forever more. This is MY Word, MY Message. Share MY Love. Show the lost MY Love.

I Love you dear bride. Do not lose hope in this dark world.

Your BRIDEGROOM Cometh!

I AM HE—LIGHT EVERLASTING

The CHRIST

YAHUSHUA!

Coordinating Scripture:

Romans 1:16-17(KJV):16For I am not ashamed of the Gospel of CHRIST: for it is the Power of GOD unto salvation to everyone that believeth; to the Jew first, and also to the Greek. 17For therein is the Righteousness of GOD revealed from faith to faith: as it is written, The just shall live by faith.

Psalm 121:7-8(KJV):7The LORD shall preserve thee from all evil: HE shall preserve thy soul. 8The LORD shall preserve thy going out and thy coming in from this time forth, and even for evermore.

Matthew 25:8(KJV): And the foolish said unto the wise, Give us of your oil; for our lamps are gone out.

Philippians 2:8(KJV): And being found in fashion as a man, HE humbled HIMSELF, and became obedient unto death, even the death of the cross.

Romans 10:13(KJV): For whosoever shall call upon the Name of the LORD shall be saved.

Luke 11:9(KJV): And I say unto you, Ask, and it shall be given you; seek, and ye shall find; knock, and it shall be opened unto you.

John 14:3(KJV):And if I go and prepare a place for you, I will come again, and receive you unto MYSELF; that where I am, there ye may be also.

54. THE LUKEWARM CHURCHES' DESIRE TO CLING TO THE WORLD WILL BE ITS UNDOING

(Words Received from Our LORD by Susan, June 22, 2014)

It is time to take a new Letter:

Children, this is your GOD, I have Words to give you.

This is the hour to sit up and pay attention. There is a growing concern: evil is moving swiftly throughout the earth. Light is the only thing moving faster: MY LIGHT, MY TRUTH pierces out into the darkness. MY TRUTH breaks down the darkness. There is NO other truth but MY TRUTH—NO other place to turn.

Soon the darkness will overwhelm MY TRUTH when the RESTRAINER is taken out of the way: MY HOLY SPIRIT WHO is inside MY bride. She will be raptured with MY SPIRIT intact and the "left behind" church will function with only half-full lamps. MY TRUTH will not shine as brightly with MY bride missing from the earth. Although I AM OMNIPRESENT, the earth will be missing the humans who possess FULL oil lamps at the time of the removal of the church, MY bride, to the Heavenlies. She, combined with the FULLNESS of The HOLY SPIRIT is what keeps the present world in check. It is by the Power she wields: the prayers of the true saints who pray by the Power of The HOLY SPIRIT FULLY SURRENDERED to CHRIST and FULLY submitted to the Will of GOD that holds back the evil forces of darkness around the whole earth.

Without MY SPIRIT and MY bride, this world will witness true darkness like never before. The lukewarm church will remain to fend for itself in a very dark world. The lukewarm church will then know the meaning of its weakened position with GOD…its lackluster faith…its denial of its need for MY SPIRIT in its midst. The lukewarm will then long for the very thing it had so long rejected: the Power of MY HOLY SPIRIT.

It is in its "left behind" condition that the lukewarm church will come to terms with the error of its thinking: its desire to handle GOD and the world simultaneously, to attempt to blend the things of GOD with the world and its ways. The lukewarm churches' desire to cling to the world will be its undoing.

The lukewarm church will have to make its way back to ME through the hands' of MY enemy. There will be NO other way of escape. The darkest hour of humanity is coming…

You can avoid this hour that is coming to the earth. Surrender yourself to your LORD and MASTER: CHRIST. There is NO other way—NO other answer—NO other means of escape.

Repent, forgive all others, surrender your life and will to ME, your LORD. Pull yourself away from the corruption of the lukewarm church, the church that knows ME NOT.

This is your LORD and SAVIOR,

The ONE TRUE HOPE

Coordinating Scripture:

John 8:12(KJV): Then spake JESUS again unto them, saying, I AM The LIGHT of the world: he that followeth ME shall not walk in darkness, but shall have the LIGHT of Life.

2 Thessalonians 2:7 (KJV): For the mystery of iniquity doth already work: only HE WHO now letteth will let, until HE be taken out of the way.

Matthew 25:10 (KJV): And while they went to buy, the BRIDEGROOM came; and they that were ready went in with HIM to the marriage: and the door was shut.

Ephesians 6:12 (KJV): For we wrestle not against flesh and blood, but against principalities, against powers, against the rulers of the darkness of this world, against spiritual wickedness in high places.

Revelation 3:16 (KJV): So then because thou art lukewarm, and neither cold nor hot, I will spue thee out of MY Mouth.

2 Timothy 3:5 (KJV): Having a form of godliness, but denying the power thereof: from such turn away.

Revelation 22:17 (KJV): And the SPIRIT and the bride say, Come. And let him that heareth say, Come. And let him that is athirst come. And whosoever will, let him take the WATER of Life freely.

55. TESTIMONIES OF ENCOUNTERS WITH GOD

Dear Followers of CHRIST:

In this writing, I have included three separate testimonies of encounters with GOD (including my own testimony) that led each individual to deep and intense remorse over past and present sinfulness. The Bible says this: Hebrews 10:31 (KJV): It is a fearful thing to fall into the hands of The Living GOD. Even in this Scripture you see that CHRIST had a Spirit of the knowledge and fear of the LORD: Isaiah 11:1-3 (NIV): A SHOOT will come up from the stump of Jesse; from his roots a BRANCH will bear fruit. 2 The SPIRIT of The LORD will rest on HIM—the Spirit of wisdom and of understanding, the Spirit of counsel and of might, the Spirit of the knowledge and fear of The LORD—3 and HE will delight in the fear of The LORD. I hope these testimonies speak to your heart and you understand the importance of seeking GOD with submission and a genuine fear for GOD:

–Othusitse Mmusi from the book "Revelations of Heaven and Hell"

Ever since I was very young, I sensed the call of GOD upon my life, and I gave my life to JESUS!! As far as I remember, I loved GOD from a very young and tender age. I used to have some dreams, visions, and revelations of The LORD, I saw angels, I saw the glory of GOD, had several dreams of JESUS CHRIST, but then I backslid as I reached my teenage years, going into alcohol, filthy relationships, and the world. It continued for something like five years, but then in the year 2010, The LORD had to intervene to stop my madness. HE arrested me on the road while going to buy something. So in my backslidden state, I went and spread myself on the floor before GOD, then came to me a huge conviction of the HOLY GHOST. It was so much that I wept for hours. I felt how sinful

170

I was that I had broken the Heart of GOD. 2 Corinthians 7:10:For godly sorrow worketh repentance to salvation not to be repented of: but the sorrow of the world worketh death. That's how GOD saved my life from sin, the world, and Spiritual death (Romans 6:23). After so much crying and GODLY sorrow, I felt so much relieved, much lighter. I had just gotten born again or restored back to The LORD by The HOLY SPIRIT.

–Charles Finney, Evangelist

There was no light in the room; nevertheless, it appeared to me as if it were perfectly light. As I went in and shut the door after me, it seemed to me as if I met the LORD JESUS CHRIST FACE-to-face. It did not occur to me then nor did it for some time afterwards, that it was a wholly-mental state. On the contrary, it seemed to me that I saw Him as I would see any other man. HE said nothing, but looked at me in such a manner as to break me right down at HIS Feet…it seemed to me a reality that HE stood before me and I fell down at HIS Feet and poured out my soul to HIM. I wept aloud like a child and made such confessions as I could with a choked utterance. It seemed to me that I bathed HIS Feet with tears, and yet I had no distinct impression that I touched HIM.

–Susan Davis, from the Book "In Love with the Whirlwind"

While alone in my bedroom, I was reading someone else's personal account of the holiness of GOD. Something about this person's account of GOD truly convicted me. Even though I did not see any bright lights or anyone at all, suddenly without warning there was an overwhelming presence of GOD, which I have never experienced before in my life. Without any thought about what I was doing, I threw myself flat on the ground and then I wept and wept with agony and was exceedingly remorseful. At that point, I caught a small glimpse of the incredible and awesome holiness of GOD and I simultaneously grasped the horror of my own lack of holiness. I recalled many of the things I had done in my past that had never previously struck me as being any problem or even a big deal. There really are not words to describe the deep anguish I experienced over the realization of my miserable sinful past. I literally felt that I was ruined. In addition, these were thoughts that came to my mind—ruination—such ruin—such remorse—regret—utter ruin. I knew I was near a Holy GOD and there was nothing good about me at all. I despaired greatly over my horribleness. The experience was staggering and I really have no earthly explanation for it. But after such great remorse set in over my horrible past, I felt a great sense of peace—the kind you feel after a storm comes through and the way you feel after the rain has stopped and there is a fresh spring feeling in the air. I felt that kind of incredible peace.

56. YOUR HEART NEEDS TO BE BEATING FOR ME

(Words Received from Our LORD by Susan, July 21, 2014)

Let ME give you a New Letter:

Children, I am Coming! This is MY Promise. This is your blessing IF you are WATCHING—IF you are LOOKING. I am coming on the clouds. I will be riding on a white stallion.

You need to be WATCHING. Your heart needs to be beating for ME. If you do not WATCH—you will miss ME in all MY GLORY—in MY Triumphant Return for MY church that I will remove in a Blaze of Glory—in the twinkling of an eye!

It's coming! I AM COMING! Don't miss this event: the Greatest Event—the Marriage Supper of The LAMB to HIS glorious bride: the church—the Union of the family of GOD to its MAKER. This event will not be replayed. It is a One-Time Event. If you miss it—you will not have another chance to be part of this Glorious Celebration—this Wedding Party!

Do not trivialize the hour you live in and think it insignificant. Your lack of concern and interest will leave you out in the cold: to face MY opponent in tribulation or to "sudden destruction." Do not mock MY Warnings. These Words are serious. They were serious before and they are now.

Your time is running out to make your pledge to your GOD to choose to be part of the Great Wedding Party. MY Love is for MY Betrothed—all others will be left to face destruction. This is your hour of decision. Will you decide for GOD or the enemy of GOD? Only you can decide to come out with ME. Clean your garments and make ready.

This is the BRIDEGROOM of the Chosen

Coordinating Scripture:

Revelation 19:11-15 (KJV): 11 And I saw heaven opened, and behold a white horse; and HE that sat upon him was called FAITHFUL and TRUE, and in righteousness HE doth judge and make war. 12 HIS Eyes were as a flame of fire, and on HIS Head were many crowns; and HE had a name written, that no man knew, but HE HIMSELF. 13 And HE was clothed with a vesture dipped in blood: and HIS Name is called The WORD of GOD. 14 And the armies which were in Heaven followed HIM upon white horses, clothed in fine linen, white and clean. 15 And out of HIS Mouth goeth a sharp sword, that with it HE should smite the nations: and HE shall rule them with a rod of iron: and HE Treadeth the winepress of the fierceness and wrath of ALMIGHTY GOD.

Mark 13:34-37 (KJV): 34 For the SON of Man is as a man taking a far journey, who left his house, and gave authority to his servants, and to every man his work, and commanded the porter to watch. 35 Watch ye therefore: for ye know not when the master of the house cometh, at even, or at midnight, or at the cockcrowing, or in the morning: 36 Lest coming suddenly he find you sleeping. 37 And what I say unto you I say unto all, Watch.

Revelation 16:15 (KJV): Behold, I come as a thief. Blessed is he that watcheth, and keepeth his garments, lest he walk naked, and they see his shame.

1 Thessalonians 5:3 (KJV): For when they shall say, Peace and safety; then sudden destruction cometh upon them, as travail upon a woman with child; and they shall not escape.

Matthew 22:14 (KJV): For many are called, but few are chosen.

57. I AM A GOD WHO IS IN LOVE WITH HIS CHILDREN

(Words Received from Our LORD by Susan, July 22, 2014)

Dear Children:

This is your LORD. I have Words to give you. I am a GOD WHO is in Love with HIS children. I Love MY children so much, I want you to obey ME—to follow MY Ways—to surrender yourselves to ME—to submit to MY Will apart from your own will. You must trust ME in this…that I KNOW BEST…that I WILL DELIVER you to a good ending…that MY Plans are Superior to your plans: your plans forged in the dark.

You cannot see up ahead the way your GOD, your MAKER can. I KNOW ALL—I SEE ALL. You must come to know ME…to trust ME…to relinquish ALL to ME—every bit of who you are including your own future plans.

Try though you may, all your far-fetched planning cannot make your future plans come to pass. Why can't you see this? It is evil to think otherwise. This is the way of the pagan, the heathen, to disregard GOD and conceive plans apart from ME—The ALL POWERFUL—ALL SEEING GOD. I AM The GOD of the future. I know what lies ahead. I am The MAKER of the future. To put your heart, soul, mind, and strength into your own planning is foolish. It is blind-sighted evil scheming against the Will of GOD—against the Kingdom of GOD. Should you continue in this vain pursuit, you will have blood on your hands—the blood of those I could have saved through you, if you would have moved in MY Precious ALL-SEEING—ALL-KNOWING Will—the Will for your life and the Will for others I am able to reach through your life.

To walk in your own will apart from MY Will for your life is wicked and prideful. You belong to the enemy and the good you think you are accomplishing is not MY Good. It is a ruse to make you think you are right with ME. The good you plan on your own apart from ME will burn up in the end and will not be rewarded by ME or remembered. Make sure you are surrendered to MY Will.

You must surrender your ALL to ME—repent and surrender your heart, soul, mind, and your future plans to your LORD and CAPTAIN. I AM HE. There is no other. Come before ME and make things right between US before the world is completely turned over to evil and before I Remove MY true followers: MY bride.

You are operating on borrowed time apart from MY Will. Step into MY Will—it is the ONLY safe place to be.

These Warnings are from Above given to you with Love from your MAKER,

CHRIST The LORD

Coordinating Scripture:

1 Peter 4:17 (KJV): For the time is come that judgment must begin at the house of GOD: and if it first begin at us, what shall the end be of them that obey not the gospel of GOD?

James 4:7-8 (KJV): 7Submit yourselves therefore to GOD. Resist the devil, and he will flee from you. 8 Draw nigh to GOD, and HE will draw nigh to you. Cleanse your hands, ye sinners; and purify your hearts, ye double minded.

James 4:13-14 (KJV): 13 Go to now, ye that say, Today or tomorrow we will go into such a city, and continue there a year, and buy and sell, and get gain: 14 Whereas ye know not what shall be on the morrow. For what is your life? It is even a vapour, that appeareth for a little time, and then vanisheth away.

Matthew 7:21 (KJV): Not everyone that saith unto ME, LORD, LORD, shall enter into the Kingdom of Heaven; but he that doeth the Will of MY FATHER which is in Heaven.

58. THIS IS A LOST GENERATION - PURSUING ALL OTHER THINGS BESIDES ITS GOD

(Words Received from Our LORD by Susan, September 6, 2014)

Daughter, Let US begin:

Children, this is your LORD speaking—I am coming to get MY bride out of this evil world—she loves ME above all else. She is clear-minded and knows the path I have set her on—the straight and narrow path. Very few want to find this path. The lost are on the broad road that leads to great loss—eternal death—hell and torment.

I am LIFE children—without ME—there is NO life. The world seeks after answers apart from ME—but I AM the ANSWER to all the ills and evils of this world. Very few seek after the right answers—the answers I am more than eager to give those who choose ME and pursue ME with all their heart and soul. This is the bride. She is watching, waiting, seeking, and finding her GOD.

I do not hide from those who pursue ME with great ferocity. I seek those who want to know ME—who really want to KNOW their MAKER. Few care to inquire of ME WHO I AM and what I am about and what it means to them. Few care to travel this path of daily seeking ME—reading MY Word, talking to ME, and exalting ME in their heart. What a sad state of affairs—for MY Own creation to reject ME and to disengage from MY Presence.

This is a lost generation—pursuing all other things besides its GOD. This generation is dying. They are steeped in evil—they wear it across their chests like a banner. They are plummeting into the depths of depravity. Most do not see the error of their ways: they are too far gone, too far into their sin to notice how ugly they have become. There is little hope for this lost generation. So many will travel the broad road to hell and align themselves with my enemy. The enemy is only too happy to drag them under. This is his delight.

Children, you were made to carry MY Light. Come and fill your oil lamps before it is too late. Come and request of ME a full oil lamp. Don't wait too long. Filling your lamp at the time of MY arrival will be too late. I will not acknowledge you—even a half-full oil lamp will not be enough.

Do you know what a full oil lamp is? It is a full surrender—a completely empty heart crying out to be filled with MY SPIRIT— dying to self. Ready to let MY SPIRIT come in and take over, to make ME LORD and MASTER over your life. Your casual attempts to have me in your life will not fill your lamp. A partial filling will not light your way—the scales on your eyes will block your vision and keep you in the dark. You will continue to grope in the dark grasping onto all other kinds of unprofitable false teachings that will lead you astray. This is what happens when you run apart from ME—you are misled and if you don't change your course direction and come back to the Narrow Path aided by a full oil lamp you will be lost for eternity on the broad way that leads to destruction.

You must really want this directional change for your life. It must be the desire of your heart. You must truly want it. Don't wait too long— many will have this change of heart after the bride is removed. Then this desire will be great, but it will be too late to escape the enemy who remains behind to torment the left behind church. Turn back to ME now—escape great sorrow, the sadness of a world completely lost without its GOD. That's what is coming.

I am waiting to receive you into the Kingdom. But, I cannot wait forever.

This is the SAVIOR of the World: MIGHTY to SAVE

Coordinating Scripture:

Matthew 7:14 (KJV): Because strait is the gate, and narrow is the way, which leadeth unto life, and few there be that find it.

Matthew 25:8-12 (KJV): 8 And the foolish said unto the wise, Give us of your oil; for our lamps are gone out. 9 But the wise answered, saying, Not so; lest there be not enough for us and you: but go ye rather to them that sell, and buy for yourselves. 10 And while they went to buy, the bridegroom came; and they that were ready went in with him to the marriage: and the door was shut. 11 Afterward came also the other virgins, saying, Lord, Lord, open to us. 12 But he answered and said, Verily I say unto you, I know you not.

Matthew 7:13 (KJV):13 Enter ye in at the strait gate: for wide is the gate, and broad is the way, that leadeth to destruction, and many there be which go in thereat:

Acts 9:17-18 (KJV):17 And Ananias went his way, and entered into the house; and putting his hands on him said, Brother Saul, the LORD, even JESUS, that appeared unto thee in the way as thou camest, hath sent me, that thou mightest receive thy sight, and be filled with the HOLY GHOST. 18 And immediately there fell from his eyes as it had been scales: and he received sight forthwith, and arose, and was baptized.

Psalm 81:12 (KJV): So I gave them up unto their own hearts' lust: and they walked in their own counsels.

59. SACREDNESS OF THE NAME OF GOD

Transcript of Donna McDonald's Presentation given at The LORD's End Time Prophecy Conference, August 16, 2014, Indianapolis, IN—SACREDNESS OF THE NAME OF GOD (and also follow up confirmations given by Susan Davis):

I read my Bible Sunday morning August 3, 2014, upstairs as I like to do first thing when I wake up. Then I went down stairs and with my head covered and kneeling I prayed and said to the LORD, "You know my heart and you know my limitations and you know the needs of the people. Please give me a message for them." And in tongues which I could not distinguish and with great fervor the HOLY SPIRIT took over and prayed a most energetic and egregious and exceptional prayer for you for some time. HE was emphatic. I had absolutely no idea what HE was going to say. I get excited to hear what the HOLY SPIRIT is going to give to me to speak when I go to a conference. HE normally says very beautiful and amazing and loving things. What HE is saying here is very serious and I was in shock when I heard HIM speak. Here are the Words the LORD is saying to you, all of you not only conference goers, following this appeal to HIS FATHER by the power of the HOLY SPIRIT. Here is what HE has to say to you:

MY children, this is the LORD speaking. I AM your FATHER and Friend. I AM the Best Thing that ever happened to you. When I died on the cross late in that day on the hill of Golgotha and gave up MY GHOST to MY FATHER and drew MY Last Breath I became the very Best Thing that ever happened to you. But I want to tell you one or more things and that is: the world is mocking their GOD and

180

is making a bed of thorns to lie onto and to go down a slippery slope into the depth of hell for themselves.

The world is an enmity to ME. I have given MY Life and MY ALL to the world, my children of the world, and they stand in line to pay to have ME mocked. They do it every time they go to a movie theater with the exception of very few movies, GOD is NOT DEAD being one example. They do it most every time they open a book and most every time they turn on the TV, every billboard, every notice in the newspaper, every salutation. and explanation. Most every one of these times the people who I call MY children open their mouths and out of it comes something unholy and mocking to their GOD, ME. I can no longer tolerate this. How long would your earthly father tolerate a mouth that is mocking and disrespectful and ugly and sinful pointed towards him? How many times would your earthly mother I have given you, sit aside and watch their own sons and daughters ruin their lives? Well, I am a GOD that can tolerate none of this anymore. I have had enough. I have had it up to MY Eyebrows and MY FATHER who knows everyone's heart is hearing it and smelling the stench in the throne room and HE has had enough. WE are your FATHER and WE are ready to give you all a good spanking. WE are ready to get out the rod and spank the world and the people in it for the disrespect that my daughter and her ears and MY Ears and MY FATHER's Ears have had to listen to. I have given this daughter a desire for clean and wholesome and holy talk and she has been privy to all of you children who call ME by Name and call ME your FATHER but you insist on using omg and oh my gosh and golly and g--d-- and the like. I have had enough of it and I am ready to get out the rod and give you all a spanking even those who call yourselves MY bride. Shame on you, children, get out the soap tonight and place it in your own mouth. Every one of you have soap in your hotel rooms and every one of you have soap in your homes. If your mouths were as antiseptic as your soaps I would not be having these conversations with you, children. I am your FATHER and I love you lest I let you fall into the pits of hell for blaspheming MY HOLY NAME and the NAME of MY HOLY FATHER WHO is in the Throne Room listening to this conference right now. HE has had it and will start applying the rod of discipline the next time you carelessly use MY HOLY Name in vain. You have been warned, do not come crying to ME If MY FATHER applies the rod of discipline to the seat of knowledge. I am a Loving GOD but a firm and just GOD as well. I cannot let this go on any longer. I have had it with you. AMEN, AMEN, AMEN, AMEN

Daughter you may sit down now as your responsibility to speak at this conference is over. You have been used to apply the rod of discipline to MY children. AMEN, go sit down.

In response to the Letter Donna received August 3, 2014 regarding the misuse of the LORD's HOLY NAME, her Letter from the LORD was prayed over by Susan Davis and this is what HE had to say through her August 19, 2014:

This problem of "loose lips" is deep and wide and far among church goers. They will live to regret it. The hour is coming. I will not allow this filthy church, this church that misuses MY Name to come unto ME. So many do not see the error of their way. MY Words hold no weight in their mind and heart. There is no value to what I am teaching them. They have completely given themselves over to the world that they have and embrace.

MY children you are witnessing an end of an era. This church age is about to end. I am about to call an end to it. I am about to bring out MY bride and leave the lukewarm church behind. She will then know she had blasphemed her GOD. She is MY church of ill repute. She wants to grab all MY glory and display it in all her own wicked ways.

They are not even mindful of MY Will. They walk all the way around MY Will seeking their own will. They rush to sin. They run to wickedness. They have their own filth. They fill their minds with such evil and corruption. I can no longer look upon this church. I am sickened and ill by this church that uses MY Name so coarsely. I am about to spew them out of MY mouth. I cannot take this abomination any longer.

I am a GIVER of life and death. I am HOLY, I walk HOLY. I am going to have MY Way with those who disregard ME. Their disregardful way will be met with destruction. Let this church tremble in fear. MY church must submit to ME, surrender their all and work out their salvation with fear and trembling. MY Words have not changed. They are the same today as yesterday. The church has changed but I have not changed. They have altered their ways to please themselves but I have not changed My Ways. I am still a GOD of purity and holiness and I demand respect from MY children, respect for MY Name, respect for MY Ways, respect for MY Truth. This is all in the Words I have spoken in MY book. You are a witness to MY Words. Where three are gathered together HE is in our midst. Put the Words out, make them known. I will continue to warn the harlot church.

Susan Davis prayed over this message with Donna McDonald on August 13, 2013. This is what the LORD had to say to her about the message that Donna just delivered regarding misuse of HIS HOLY NAME:

My ears burn when my children do this. It saddens and angers ME. They are so ill prepared to come into MY Glory. They must come into the light and become clean. They must clean their garments of this disgraceful filth, of this pollution of the mouth. Their words must be pleasing to ME and not offensive. MY Name must be revered, hallowed.

We asked if there are any Words Donna and I use that are displeasing to HIM. HE said: Try to refrain from even using phrases like, oh my goodness. It has a hint of using My Name... Soon after HE said this I heard 'expletive deletive' referring to these, 'oh my goodness' phrases', The LORD is angry over this misuse of HIS Holy Name. Words given from the LORD to Susan Davis, August 13, 2014-- https://www.youtube.com/watch?v=BEJ8RrZS3p

60. YOU CAN MOVE IN THE KINGDOM OF GOD WHILE ON THE EARTH BY SURRENDERING YOUR ALL

(Words Received from Our LORD by Susan, September 10, 2014)

(I had read my Bible and was talking to the LORD, just spending time with HIM one morning recently and HE started telling me these things. I said this is remarkable and I asked HIM if I should journal these Words and HE said, "Yes," and for me to get my journal. I got my journal and pen and HE started telling me what to write down. This is what HE gave me for you to hear):

Today, I want to address the change of the human during rapture into a perfect being, apart from the earthly state--the completion of the human into a state of being ready to come before GOD in HOLY Matrimony at the moment of rapture in the twinkling of an eye.

The person raptured changes. He takes on a new body. His body, a flesh body from the soil of the earth changes into a new body that comes from the soil of Heaven. This new body is fluid, it is able to change. It takes on a state of fluidity. It can change form from that of a person into light and back depending on the desires of GOD. The thoughts and desires of the person in MY Presence, living with ME are also MY Thoughts and Desires--WE are ONE in SPIRIT.

Presently, evil man's desires on earth are not MY desires--WE are not ONE. This is sin: men who are outside of MY Will walk in their own desires for their life. They are not submitted to MY Desires for their life, MY Will for their life. I am not their LORD and MASTER. This is the face of evil.

Heaven and the New Jerusalem, the dwelling place of MY bride is not like this. MY bride, fully submitted to ME on earth, operates fully in MY Desires for their life and so they are within the Kingdom of GOD, even while on the earth. This is the significance of full submission to GOD, surrendered fully to CHRIST, willfully submitted to the Will of the FATHER, possessing the fullness of the HOLY SPIRIT by humble submission moving into HOLINESS, separating from the desires of evil men, pulling away from that that is evil. This is loving your GOD with all your heart, mind, soul, and strength, and loving those around you as yourself.

You can move in the Kingdom of GOD while on the earth by surrendering your all--your earthly desires, your desires to sin apart from GOD's Desires for your life, submitted to HIS Perfect Will. Then, at the time of rapture, your human body will change instantly into an eternal body able to come into the Presence of GOD and to dwell with HIM forever.

Make this exchange of your evil plans for Kingdom plans. Turn from your sin--your evil desires apart from GOD's Desires: HOLINESS, PURITY, WHOLENESS, LOVE. This is what I want for you: to be set apart, HOLY and PURE, focused on ME, your LORD and MASTER: running in MY Ways, in MY Truths, understanding the things I value: caring about the lost, the weak, the needy, living PURE in an evil world.

Make ready for MY return, wash yourself in MY Word, come clean in MY Truth. Surrender your desires over to MY Desires. Walk in PEACE with ME, your GOD, your MAKER. All will be well between us. Without this surrender you are outside MY Eternal Kingdom, outside of MY Will, fully enslaved to MY enemy, doing his will, performing evil, working against MY Kingdom. Come and lay down your life to ME before it is too late for you to make this choice and you be cast away from MY Presence for eternity. You decide what kingdom you belong to.

This is your CREATOR

I AM The HIGHLY EXALTED KING of the Universe

Coordinating Scripture:

(The LORD gave me these specific scriptures for this letter)

Psalm 29:11: The LORD will bless HIS people with peace.

Isaiah 55:12: Ye shall go out with joy and be led forth with peace.

The Following Letter Was Given by the LORD to Donna McDonald September 12, 2014:

I love you so. When I died on the cross for you at Calvary it was the greatest act of love that a human or GOD could ever do for you. I was both Human and GOD at that moment in time.

I felt every pain and every suffering that the Roman soldiers meted out to me. I knew their every thought and saw them spat on ME and I knew what hatred they had in their heart for ME. It was all of creation--those whom I created that crucified ME. The Roman soldiers were merely pawns, puzzle pieces depicting all of human kind. They were evil, yes, but so are the hearts of all men until they meet with their GOD: ONE on one in an intimate relationship-- having received ME first then submitting to ME and pursuing ME in a FULL SUBMISSION. These are the ways of salvation then pursue the HOLY SPIRIT in a full submission having prayed to be filled with HIM. HE is the "dunamis" and the power behind every victorious Christian young or old, male or female. HE is the LIGHT that LIGHTS up the world and the Heavens through ME.

When you come into Heaven you will be illuminated by LIGHT and you will be a very fluid being changing and altering to meet MY needs for you. We will have a supernatural relationship ONE on one that will go on for eternity. I will be able to know and feel your every thought and emotion as well and you will be tapped into ME supernaturally as well. This is a very beautiful thing that MY FATHER has set up and created for you in Heaven.

You will be dazzled by the display of HIS creation and the life and the beauty in Heaven. This is the amazing place and beyond your wildest and most creative imagination. Do not hither and do not tarry. Get right with ME today or you will be right with the enemy. Accept ME as your LORD and SAVIOR. Give ME a full submission including giving over all your hopes, plans and dreams and interests and relationships. I will take over your life when you are completely submitted to ME and make you into the person you were created to be. This is a true statement. Then accept the HOLY SPIRIT in HIS complete filling and this will provide the "dunamis" you need to overcome sin.

This is a complete and lasting relationship for eternity. It is only an arm's length away. Reach out your arm and take MY Hand and I will lead you to the greatest possibilities you could ever imagine and more for I am your KING and EVERLASTING LORD. ALLELUIA, AMEN, AMEN, AMEN, AMEN.

I am told I am to include with this message from the LORD to Donna McDonald, September 10, 2014:

Children, listen, there is a darkness coming over the earth, it is called ISIS. It is evil in the nth degree. It is evil multiplied. It is from the enemy, straight from the mouth of hell. My children must pray against this and pray that they will be served worthy to be brought off the earth in the rapture. Pray that your soul will be saved from this darkness over the earth before it spreads like wildfire. AMEN, AMEN, AMEN, AMEN

61. WHAT THE LUKEWARM CHURCH WON'T TELL YOU

I asked the LORD about the problem with the lukewarm church:

They do not pursue ME as their FIRST LOVE."

• Revelation 2:4 (KJV): Nevertheless I have somewhat against thee, because thou hast left thy FIRST LOVE.

• They do not hold ME in a place of honor in their hearts

• Deuteronomy 13:3 (KJV): Thou shalt not hearken unto the words of that prophet, or that dreamer of dreams: for The LORD your GOD proveth you, to know whether ye love The LORD your GOD with all your heart and with all your soul.

• They are irreverent in their treatment of what I consider "HOLY":

• MY Holy Name

• Leviticus 22:2 (KJV): Speak unto Aaron and to his sons, that they separate themselves from the holy things of the children of Israel, and that they profane not MY Holy Name in those things which they hallow unto ME: I am the LORD.

• They are irreverent in their treatment of what I consider "HOLY":

MY Holy Sanctuary:

• Leviticus 26:2 (KJV): Ye shall keep MY Sabbaths, and reverence MY Sanctuary: I am the LORD.

• They are irreverent in their treatment of what I consider "HOLY":

• MY Holy Sabbath

• Leviticus 26:2 (KJV): Ye shall keep MY Sabbaths, and reverence MY Sanctuary: I am the LORD,

• They are irreverent in their treatment of what I consider "HOLY":

• MY Holy Laws

• Matthew 5:17 (KJV): Think not that I am come to destroy the law, or the prophets: I am not come to destroy, but to fulfill.

• They are irreverent in their treatment of what I consider "HOLY":

• MY Holy Name

• MY Holy Sanctuary

• MY Holy Sabbath

• MY Holy Laws

• MY people have turned against that which I consider "HOLY" and have mixed the "HOLY" with the world so the people no longer recognize the "HOLY."

This is the trouble with the people—they lack respect. They are rebellious and want their own ways, their own wills. They want the world, the fleshly. They want to handle evil, look upon evil, touch and feel it, and then to return to ME as if there is no problem in engaging with evil and coming and going from MY Presence as if I will tolerate their loose handling of evil with MY "HOLINESS." This is the desire of the Lukewarm Church: to attempt to handle the "HOLY" and to play with evil."

They give evil a "wink" and their hearts barely blush by the choice of the things they watch and read. They look the other way at evil—no one takes up for the widows and fatherless, the poor and the weak. It's every man for himself: no one cares to pursue his neighbor for ME."

Ezra 9:6 (KJV): And said, O my GOD, I am ashamed and blush to lift up my face to thee, my GOD: for our iniquities are increased over our head, and our trespass is grown up unto the heavens.

The Lukewarm Church does not value MY Laws and Ways. I extend grace, but MY Grace does not promote adultery, lust, and the pursuit of idol worship. The church believes that grace is easy access between evil and GOD: play with the world freely and have GOD when you need HIM."

This is MY Lukewarm Church: they clutch evil in one hand and attempt to clutch ME in the other. They fool themselves. They are only clutching evil…because I am an ALL or nothing GOD and those who cling to the world and pursue ME will be disappointed when they stand before ME. I will tell them to depart from ME. They will learn then what their tepid belief in ME means to ME."

"They are looking under every rock for answers. But I have ALL the answers. I am The ONE who can cure all their ills…"

Transcript from the Prayer in the Presentation "What the Lukewarm Church Won't Tell You" /Presenter: Susan Davis--The LORD's End

191

Times Prophecy Conference--August 16, 2014: Powerpoint Notes provided upon request/kidsmktg@sbcglobal.net

If you are willing—pray with me today:

LORD: I repent of being lukewarm—and chasing after worldly "emptiness."

I repent of having a "lackluster" faith

I repent for trusting in the pursuit of the world's answers for my life instead of GOD's Will for my life

I repent for giving my precious GOD-given time to the world instead of MY MAKER WHO gives me my every breath and determines my eternal outcome.

I repent for lusting after the temporal thrill of the world in lieu of pursuing an intimate relationship with my MAKER

I repent for being in the Will of the enemy instead of walking in the Will of the Divine.

I repent for arrogantly doing good outside of the Divine Will of GOD and thinking my will is best.

I repent for denying the POWER of the HOLY SPIRIT to enter MY LIFE so that I can walk in the WILL of GOD and to conquer sin and pursue holiness.

LORD: I want to be in your DIVINE WILL and not my own

I want to possess your HOLY SPIRIT in FULL MEASURE

I want to have a FULL OIL LAMP so that when you return for your bride you will see me

I want to pursue holiness and walk in truth

I want to find and stay on the narrow path that few find

I want to be assured a place with you for all eternity

I want to know CHRIST as an intimate friend

I want to experience mental wholeness and stability and live in peace with my MAKER

I open my heart up to you LORD JESUS—be my ALL in All…And ALL GOD's People say AMEN!

62. KNOWING THE HOUR WE LIVE IN

This Special Edition focuses on Christians "Knowing the Hour We Live in."

When you read Exodus about the plagues of Egypt that GOD sent to convince the Pharaoh to release the Israelites, most people probably scratch their heads and wonder—how could anyone be so stubborn as that guy was? How could anyone just keep rejecting the request of Moses to "Let GOD's people go?" Well the Bible says this in Exodus 7:3 (KJV): And I will harden Pharaoh's heart, and multiply MY signs and MY wonders in the land of Egypt.

So GOD hardened Pharaoh's heart to the many signs and wonders GOD sent to him. The Pharaoh in Exodus is a kind of "Lukewarm

Christian" of today. Over and over the "end time" signs lining up with the Bible are going on RIGHT NOW—and the lukewarm church is behaving the same way. Are you like Pharaoh? Are you one of those that GOD said HE would harden in Romans 9:18?

Romans 9:17-18 (KJV): For the scripture saith unto Pharaoh, Even for this same purpose have I raised thee up, that I might shew MY Power in thee, and that MY Name might be declared throughout all the earth. 18 Therefore hath HE mercy on whom HE will have mercy, and whom HE will HE hardeneth.

Read and watch the messages below about the irrefutable proof that we are now living in the end times and now is the time to make ready for the LORD's Return for HIS church.

(Taken from the article below—"Stop Deceiving People About the End Times")

Not only are the "end times" signs coming to pass which signal that this generation should be watching and on guard...the Christians who won't embrace this message are not looking at the true challenge of "not a moment too soon" to be telling the "end time" message:

Here is the dilemma (formula), fellow Christians: massive population + (plus) short amount of time remaining: however long that may be (based on the rapid number of end time signs coming about simultaneously) + (plus) the requirements of GOD for the removal of the church—holiness/purity/wrinkle-free/spotless robes/full oil lamp + (plus) major "worldly" distractions from a ruthless enemy = (equals) recipe for disaster: many, many ill-prepared, non-informed people—caught off guard, unsuspecting, and left behind!

63. A DANCE WITH THE DEVIL IS A DANCE WITH DEATH

(Words Received from Our LORD by Susan, September 23, 2014)

My daughter I am ready to give you Words. Children, this is your LORD Speaking:

There is confusion in the world, it centers on evil, evil that rules and reigns over mankind for the hearts of men have turned to evil. All their thoughts are of continuous evil, that which is apart from GOD. This world knows no boundaries for evil. It is turning toward the side of darkness in all its ways. How can I bless such a world? How can I bring MY blessing to such a world? I cannot. I am a GOD of Truth. I have given MY precepts, MY commandments and the world refuses to acknowledge them. The world would rather pursue madness, corruption, evil, and run from its' GOD to all that is sinful.

Children, I must come soon and remove the remnant who truly want to walk away from evil and the ways of the world-to be set apart, unique from the ways of the world. Very few want this alternative. Most embrace all that is in the world and never inquire of ME, GOD, CREATOR of their being.

Once I claim MY beloved out of the world to safety, I will turn and deal with this evil world that so shuns ME, MY Ways, MY Truth. The enemy will have free reign over the entire earth to do as he pleases. It will be a hostile environment for all left to contend with it.

The world is only now sampling what is yet to come: a world without GOD's Hand to secure and guard and maintain the sanctity of life. Life will not be of value in the hands of MY enemy once I pull MY bride free of its grasp. This day is coming. Prepare your hearts, your garments: make ready.

Many feel they can wait and that playing with the world is still a safe position. Don't be so sure of yourself. MY children fall away every day. You are never safe as long as you cling to the world, MY enemy, your ways—outside of a full surrender to MY Will and MY Blood Covering. Without this full surrender you are outside of MY full protection. I am not a GOD that you can dabble or play with. I do not take lightly to half-way commitments. This is an abomination to ME and what I stand for.

A dance with the devil is a dance with death. Be careful how much dancing you do. When I come for MY church the music will stop on earth and your days of dancing will end. Let these Words resonate through your spirit. Turn wholly to your GOD before it is too late.

This is the HOLY ONE ABOVE

Coordinating Scripture:

Genesis 6:5 (KJV): And GOD saw that the wickedness of man was great in the earth, and that every imagination of the thoughts of his heart was only evil continually.

1 John 2:3 (KJV): And hereby we do know that we know HIM, if we keep HIS Commandments.

64. YOU MUST CHOOSE BETWEEN DEATH AND LIFE - ALL IS A CHOICE

(Words Received from Our LORD by Susan, September 24, 2014)

MY Children, it is I your LORD—

The world is in a state of confusion—the world is coming apart—there is a wind of death blowing—it is carrying evil throughout the world. MY enemy is coming into his rule and reign. This is what happens when the world rejects its GOD.

You must choose between death and life—all is a choice—the Will of GOD or the will of the devil: there are only two choices. Most choose death—their own will—the will of the enemy against the Will of GOD. What path will you choose—what direction will you move in?

The world is falling in on itself—soon it will be unrecognizable as evil will rule the land and anything that is godly will fall to the wayside. There is not much time left now. You have to decide—what direction will you move in? Will you repent of your sin—seek MY Face—surrender your all to ME, your GOD? Or will you continue on your path of destruction? You are walking on the road of sin from the time you are born until you choose to come into the Will of GOD by way of repentance and surrender to ME, your LORD and SAVIOR and MASTER.

Without MY Blood Covering you will not be found guiltless when you come before MY FATHER, MY SPIRIT, and I and your sin will condemn you to eternal hell apart from your MAKER. There is no other way to stand before a HOLY GOD—there is no other solution to your sin problem. You must work out your Salvation with fear and trembling—lay down your life before ME—acknowledge that you need a SAVIOR.

I will SAVE you—but you must confess MY Name and surrender to the Will of GOD with a sincere repentance of past sin. You must pursue ME, your GOD with all of your heart, soul, mind, and strength. These are the keys to being ready to enter MY Kingdom. Without childlike faith no one will see the Kingdom of GOD—only those who seek ME with the eyes of a child will have the faith to understand what GOD has to share through the Word, the SPIRIT, and the Heart of your GOD. There is NO OTHER path—all others lead to disaster. Render your heart to ME—Believe FULLY in ME—Turn and face ME as your Only HOPE. This is the Narrow WAY. Come and learn of the humble ways of GOD. I await your decision. Time is short—make your Way to ME now!

The desire of MY Heart is to give you Salvation—THIS is your SAVIOR—Don't deny ME this pleasure.

Coordinating Scriptures:

Matthew 7:21 (KJV): Not every one that saith unto ME, LORD, LORD, shall enter into the Kingdom of Heaven; but he that doeth the Will of MY FATHER which is in Heaven.

Matthew 18:3 (KJV): And said, Verily I say unto you, Except ye be converted, and become as little children, ye shall not enter into the Kingdom of Heaven.

Matthew 10:32 (KJV): Whosoever therefore shall confess ME before men, him will I confess also before MY FATHER which is in Heaven.

Acts 2:38 (KJV): Then Peter said unto them, Repent, and be baptized every one of you in the Name of JESUS CHRIST for the remission of sins, and ye shall receive the gift of the HOLY GHOST.

Signs That We Are Living In The "End Times":

ASTOUNDING: SIGNS IN THE EARTH BENEATH; BLOOD:

Acts 2:19-21 (KJV):19 And I will shew wonders in heaven above, and SIGNS IN THE EARTH BENEATH; BLOOD, and fire, and vapour of smoke: 20 The sun shall be turned into darkness, and the moon into blood, before the great and notable day of the Lord come: 21 And it shall come to pass, that whosoever shall call on the Name of the LORD shall be saved.

Revelation 16:4(KJV): And the third angel poured out his vial upon the rivers and fountains of waters; and they became blood.

Prepare for the very soon rapture.

Read all the books by Susan Davis :

Ready For Rapture

Bride of Christ – Prepare Now !

Left Behind After The Rapture

Rapture or Tribulation

Marriage Supper of the Lamb

Also by Susan Davis and Sabrina De Muynck

I Am Coming, Volume 1

I Am Coming, Volume 2

I Am Coming, Volume 3

I Am Coming, Volume 4

I Am Coming, Volume 5

I Am Coming, Volume 6

Available as paperbacks and kindle ebooks at:
www.amazon.com

Also available for free as ebooks (various formats) at:
www.smashwords.com

35243981R00114

Made in the USA
Charleston, SC
01 November 2014